D1403490

Time's Tapestry

Time's Tapestry

Four Generations of a New Orleans Family

LETA WEISS MARKS

LOUISIANA STATE UNIVERSITY PRESS   *Baton Rouge and London*

Designer: Michele Myatt Quinn
Typeface: Adobe Caslon
Typesetter: Impressions Book and Journal Services, Inc.
Printer and binder: Thomson-Shore, Inc.

All photographs are from the author's personal collection.

Library of Congress Cataloging-in-Publication Data

Marks, Leta Weiss, 1932–
    Time's tapestry : four generations of a New Orleans family / Leta
Weiss Marks.
        p. cm.
    Includes bibliographical references (p.   ).
    ISBN 0-8071-2205-X (cloth : alk. paper)
    1. Weiss family.   2. Dreyfous family.   3. New Orleans (La.)—
Biography.   I. Title.
CT274.W43M37   1997
976.3'3506'0922—dc21
[B]   97-25816
                                                                        CIP

B
W429
MARKS

B-143/547

The paper in this book meets the guidelines for permanence and durability of the Committee
on Production Guidelines for Book Longevity of the Council on Library Resources. ♾

To Mother, who inspired and loved our book

Contents

▼▼

*I*llustrations

$\mathcal{P}$reface

I saw in Louisiana a live-oak growing,
All alone stood it and the moss hung down from the branches,
Without any companion it grew there uttering joyous leaves of
    dark green,
And its look, rude, unbending, lusty, made me think of myself,
But I wonder'd how it could utter joyous leaves standing alone
    there without its friend near, for I knew I could not,
And I broke off a twig with a certain number of leaves upon it,
    and twined around it a little moss,
And brought it away, and I have placed it in sight in my room.
                  —Walt Whitman

Time's Tapestry: Four Generations of a New Orleans Family grew
from fragments of recollections, interviews, and research into a full-length
book—a song of myself and my family. It began several years ago, from a
particular moment during a visit to New Orleans, my childhood home, to
see my mother. While I was sitting next to Mother in her sunny bedroom
in New Orleans, abruptly she stopped talking—in the middle of a sentence.
Her head fell to one side; the pupil of that eye rolled outward to the left,
almost disappearing into its corner, while the gaze of the other pupil an-
chored itself blindly to the mauve wall.

"Mother?" I exclaimed, trying to keep from shouting hysterically, but
she didn't respond. As if a sudden sleep had arrested her, she slumped in
her chair—silent.

"Stroke," I thought, as my numb fingers found the numbers 911 on the old rotary phone.

"Yes," the doctor concurred after a hasty examination in the emergency room. "But," he added, "not a permanent one." He went on in his diagnosis, however, to warn us that it might be the prelude to a greater one. For the next few days, I sat and watched in fear as a series of small "incidents" (as they call them) followed the initial one. In between them she drifted back to me, as if awakening only from a refreshing nap.

During one of these incidents, Mother's eyes looked frozen and transfixed; they seemed to stare in amazement into the eyes of the cat with one green and one yellow eye in the painting on her bedroom wall. As I watched, petrified, she turned her still-contorted face to me and murmured something about a light and a tunnel. Unable to breathe for a moment, I stared in astonishment. Then I saw her face melt back into its former softness. Mother had returned to me from what I recognized as a near-death excursion into some mysterious other land.

Out of that moment arose the urgent need to hear.and record all that I did not know about my mother: like the victim of a famine, I hungered to learn the story of her life. Although the house she lives in is filled with bundles of photographs and letters, stashed uncataloged in drawers and albums that I had leafed through many times on visits, we had not had an intimate discussion since I left home in 1953. I had a storehouse of questions about my father, about her, and about their life together that I was eager to ask. Ever since my father's death, I have lived in Connecticut—a long way from her—too busy with studying, teaching, and child raising to think about the past. Too absorbed in time present, I had found no moment to sit and talk to her about time past. There never had been the right occasion to ask any burning questions: frantic visits to New Orleans over the years were occupied with seafood lunches, Mardi Gras parades, or journeys on the streetcar with our children to the French Quarter and the zoo. Now I saw that I had a mission: to hear and record what otherwise would be erased forever. I realized, as a result of having witnessed death touch my ninety-five-year-old mother, that she and I had been given a second chance. I had to make time wait while I gathered my mother's story, especially those parts she had kept secret—the dark moments she had hidden from me, my sister, and my brother.

In addition to what my mother could tell me, I wanted to parcel out some time as well to harvest memories and stories from Mother's ninety-three-year-old sister, Ruth. Thus, over the next two years, I traveled home to Louisiana to tap the memories of these two sisters, to preserve their lives for future generations before either one withered away.

In this book of memories and stories, I have woven a tapestry of lives and events, created from interviews with my mother and my aunt. They have told me about themselves, their recollections of other family members, and about the generation that preceded theirs. To add facts and details, I researched newspaper articles at local libraries and archives: the Historic New Orleans Collection, Touro Infirmary Archives, and Tulane University's Howard-Tilton Memorial Library—especially the Architectural Archives, which preserves my father's blueprints, drawings, and specifications. I supplemented these sources with information gleaned from documents in private collections of family members. I borrowed from letters and unpublished manuscripts, particularly those written by my father, Leon C. Weiss; my grandfather Felix J. Dreyfous; my aunt, Ruth Dreyfous; a friend, Bobbie Malone; and Tom Schwab, son of Mathilde Dreyfous (my Uncle George's wife). My bibliography lists these sources.

Throughout, I paraphrase or quote passages from the letters, primarily those written by my father, my grandfather Felix, and my great-grandfather, Abel Dreyfous. These letters have revealed to me rich details of place and have helped me know the personality of their writers. In many places, the spelling and the language, particularly my father's romantic and archaic style, carries over into my narrative passages, perhaps making my stories sound sentimental—especially the first chapter, which narrates his courting of my mother. I wanted the tales to reflect the voices and personalities of the characters in them.

Because I rely on oral and written personal accounts, letters, and conversations, the exact spelling of names was sometimes difficult to determine. Time having blurred these women's memories and yellowed the pages of handwritten letters, I found some puzzling inconsistencies in names and dates. The years, however, have not clouded perceptions and impressions that Mother and Ruth remember. From all of these primary sources, I have created my tales. Sometimes I am faithful to the real events; often I add dialogue and images. The book, then, is composed of narratives and reflections and is grounded in fact. Most of my writing comes out of the hours spent with Mother, an intimacy that grew in intensity as she and I talked, as she unraveled skeins of her life, shared letters with me that my father wrote to her during their long courtship, and as I wrote and read her story back to her. In the process of writing this work, I found myself identifying with my mother and her stories: they became my own.

The tales about family members are entwined with autobiographical passages—memories and images from my Louisiana childhood. In these sections, I tell what it was like growing up Jewish in the segregated South of the thirties and forties, and I describe my perception of the changes that have occurred over the past sixty years. I wanted also to explore the cultural and social scene in New Orleans for the three generations that preceded mine. Although I attempted through interviews and written materials to recreate their experiences, I also used secondary sources to supplement the fragments of information I gleaned from friends and relatives still living.

If I had included only journalistic renderings of the interviews, letters, recollections, journals, clippings, and histories and woven them together without my inventions to enrich them, my book would have been family history. In my narration, primary and secondary sources are fleshed out with details of landscapes and events—images created from my imagination—a medley of truth and fantasy.

In writing about my father, I found myself pondering questions about him that still remain unanswered. Naturally, he holds a special place in my memory as my daddy, but the facts about his life sit like a complex jigsaw puzzle with pieces hidden or missing. In researching, I felt compelled to find and fit them together so that I might come to terms with my ambivalence concerning events in his life. About his talent I have no doubt: his dynamic career as Huey Long's chosen architect and the spectacular buildings he designed speak to that. I have found no satisfactory explanation, however, about his role in the scandals of the time or conclusions about his innocence or guilt. Although I have learned more about him as I revisited the past and relived painful memories, my research unfolded no final truth about what happened to him. By writing I tried to find that out.

My journeys back to New Orleans, in actuality and in memory, form the warp that holds the threads together. None of the persons I write about is world famous, but some of their lives have collided with local history, even inspiring change. Some collide with close relatives and cause conflicts that are passed on to future generations. Many have lived ordinary lives; a few have aspired to greatness and power. Reaching and falling, moving and stumbling, the people in my stories illustrate human fortitude and human weakness. I write of their jealousy, courage, pain, constancy, and treachery; I unfold the drama of their interaction with one another and their conflict with social or political events and changes as I come to terms with who I am among them. They are the characters in this book. The scene is the South; the story begins in the present, flashes back to the middle of the nineteenth century, moves through the civil rights movement, and closes in the present.

In writing this book I have visited moments in time that have been precious to me. Before I wrote it, I had no idea that I was so rooted in Louisiana and that certain places there grasped me so strongly; but as I wrote, I kept returning to these special places, remembering significant events in my life. Louisiana scenes flickered before my eyes like Impressionist paintings—dreamy, muted, and yet astonishingly clear. As I remembered and wrote, I also experienced painful moments that kept me awake at night grasping for words to express them. When I first began creating details for my stories, I felt awkward—as if I were filching what did not belong to me—but that feeling soon passed as those people and events I wrote about came alive, and as I moved into their world. When I wrote about myself and my feelings, however, I did so honestly. This book has been a journey into myself as well as into the lives of others.

I wish to thank William E. Sheidley, whose confidence inspired me forward. When Bill moved from Connecticut, he left me in the competent hands of Joan Joffe Hall, whose insight and skill encouraged me onward. Other gifted professors from The University of Connecticut and from Trinity College have inspired me and given me guidance: especially Joan Hedrick, Gene Leach, James Miller, and Feenie Ziner. I am indebted to Gary Van Zante, curator of the Tulane University Architectural Archives, for his help with research.

John Easterly, managing editor of Louisiana State University Press, deserves thanks for his enthusiastic reception of my manuscript when I first submitted it and for his help throughout the various stages of publication. I want also to acknowledge my appreciation to Lawrence Powell, professor of history at Tulane, whose favorable review of my manuscript assured its acceptance at LSU Press. His recommendations encouraged me to enrich the book with deeper cultural and historical background. Finally, I want to express my gratitude to Catherine Landry, my editorial coordinator, to all the others at LSU Press who guided me through publication, and to Wendy Jacobs, my talented and meticulous copyeditor.

I wish also to acknowledge friends (particularly Michele Toomy, Cathy Kahn, and Jill Weinberger) and family members who have been patient and supportive as I vanished into my study and neglected them while I wrote. I am grateful to my husband, Alby, for his love and support; my children—Jonathan, Richard, Catherine and Alan; their spouses—Patty, Jenny, Billy, and Kathleen; my sister, Betty; my brother, Leon; their children; and my grandchildren—Sarah, Jeremy, Rachel, Hannah, Emma, Zoe, Jonah, and Jacob, for whom I wrote this book. To Ruth Dreyfous and all those too numerous to name, I give thanks. Finally, I dedicate this book to my mother, Caroline Dreyfous Weiss, the source of my inspiration.

Time's Tapestry

$\mathcal{P}$relude

We think back through mothers if we are women.
—Virginia Woolf

In journeying home to New Orleans, I always need a seat by the window of the plane in order to see the marshes, the moss-hung cypress trees, shimmering Lake Pontchartrain with its causeway and oil-rig-like structures, and of course the brown Mississippi, which holds the city within its crescent arms. As we descend through the clouds, these are the images I feel I need to see. Like the muted Drysdale scenes of live oaks and bayous painted on my mother's dining room walls, they are mysteriously beautiful in their breathless tones and shades. If we circle the city, I try to locate Audubon Park because it's close to my mother's home, the large brick house on Dominican Street my father designed and built, where I was born.

Although I have lived away from these images for more years than I lived within them, I am not a stranger but a traveler coming home each time I return. For I feel a permanence to this landscape, the city, and my childhood home that I know is only an illusion, just as I know that death will come one day to the only two of our family who still live in New Orleans—my mother and my aunt Ruth. Even though they are both in their nineties, they seem in my heart to be as enduring as the live oak trees guarding their backyards with arabesque arms.

The night sky obscured these familiar landmarks as our plane descended on this last trip in February. As we approached the main terminal from the gate, I wanted to see Mother waiting for us as she always has, but I knew that, even in her wheelchair, she could not make the effort to meet us. No familiar faces in the waiting crowd, but we knew our way. We hurried to find our luggage, and we left the terminal to find a taxi. Outside, the driveway glistened with rain, but the temperature was too cold for me to savor the tropical air that always greets me. In the cab I liked mapping directions for the driver, whose tourist passengers usually request downtown hotels—more familiar destinations for taxi drivers. He'd never heard of Dominican Street, but I could guide him there.

It was early evening—not quite seven—when we arrived, but Mother had already eaten supper, was ready for bed, and was too tired to talk that night. After sharing reports of our bumpy flight, we went downstairs, heated the gumbo that Elizabeth, her housekeeper, had prepared for us, and sat down in the dining room to sip the brown soup thick with chunks of crabmeat and shrimp. As I sat there I tried to feel my presence in this familiar room, sitting in my usual place at the table of my childhood. But here I was, having returned from my Connecticut home, where I have raised my own children, now sitting across from my husband Alby, not my sister. I looked beyond him at the bayou scene with the pirogue that Drysdale had painted with too many seats and wouldn't correct even when Daddy showed him photographs of real ones. Alexander John Drysdale, a poor but popular 1920s Louisiana artist, had painted on canvas-covered walls these scenes that Mother and Daddy had selected from the artist's sketches after giving up on finding bayou scenes in wallpaper books. Consequently, like a latter-day Giotto creating frescoes on church walls, Drysdale, perched on stepladder, painted the four walls and around and over the doors and windows of our dining room. When Daddy complained that he'd never seen a pirogue with six seats, that pirogues look more like flat-bottomed canoes than rowboats, Drysdale had answered, "Well, now you have." I looked at the wall behind the mahogany sideboard at the large landscape dominated by an oak tree sheltering a pond of water lilies. Drysdale couldn't accommodate my parents with the water hyacinths they asked for because he claimed he had never seen any, so they settled for lilies. In the background of this scene looms the fallen tree that, as a child, I believed was a train until somebody laughed and asked how a train happened to be in a landscape with too many trees and no train track. Sitting there this evening, I tried to see how I could have thought it was a train.

But the oak trees spoke to me of real ones, those guarding the lane to the pond at Kiskatom, our summer place across Lake Pontchartrain. Daddy named things there: the pond, Playzee, became a place for us to learn how male fish fan eggs in nests in shallow water, and the Tarzan Oaks, after he tied strong ropes from their branches, became climbing oaks for us to shinny up to the higher reaches of the trunk and limbs. He named the land Kiskatom, an Indian name, for the tall hickory tree next to the shell road that led to the house; Mother told me the fossil clam shells on the road once came from the sea. Our summer goal was to toughen our feet so that we could walk barefoot without pain on those shells. A grove of trees near the Tchefuncte River he named the Picnic Oaks, for there we celebrated my sister's birthdays and tried to forget the war, eating our ration of hot dogs under their mossy limbs, protected from the July Louisiana sun. Daddy planted pecan trees, blueberry bushes, tomatoes, scuppernongs, crab apples, mayhaws, and strawberries; he was forever experimenting with different plants. His effort to grow and dry peppers for paprika ended in disaster when the drying shed burned down one night. That field later became the strawberry patch.

One summer, because of Mother's passion for herbs, he helped her grow thyme, basil, and marjoram, and built racks for drying them in the attic. I liked the attic with its musty smell of drying herbs. That enterprise became a lasting one for my mother. During the war she packaged and sold blends of dried herbs, using the attic in the city for her cottage industry. I remember how she packed the jars — either in apron pockets of mammy dolls a woman made for her or nestled in Spanish moss in plain red boxes. Orders for her herbs and the cookbook she wrote with Daddy's help came from all over the world; Mother packaged them while listening to music on the radio. Soft sounds of a symphony and the pungent odor of herbs drifted down to me as I played or read in my room. Occasionally, an order will come even now from someone reading an outdated magazine advertisement.

But out there in the country, away from plans and specifications, my father's main industry was guiding children. We followed him into the cypress swamp, on a boardwalk he had built over the black water, hoping and fearing at the same time that we might see water moccasins. Daddy carried a shotgun just in case. We learned from him how to paddle a pirogue and fish with bamboo poles deep in the shadows of cypress trees on Bayou

Tête l'Ours. He showed us how, if we scraped away pine needles in the damp earth of early spring, we might find Indian Pipes, a bone-white fungus shaped like a thin-barreled gun. He told us stories at night, creating an imaginary Uncle Squiggly who lived in our woods, and comforted us when screech owls frightened us at night or when skunks left unpleasant odors below our sleeping-porch windows. He fanned our curiosity with the richness of his knowledge. He tutored us in lore and language; his naming things gave them permanence.

What darkness lay under the surface of this idyllic world? Some truths I didn't see; others I didn't understand. I knew that alligator gars lived in the Tchefuncte River, but I never saw one of those sharklike fish. When Daddy hacked off the head of a chicken for supper, I saw it run around the barnyard spouting blood from its severed neck. On the way to Madisonville to buy candy we often took a shortcut off the paved road onto the muddy footpath and passed a cluster of squalid shacks. "Niggerville," I remember my father calling it, for this was the South of the 1930s. . . .

Mother called to wish us good-night just as we finished our second bowl of gumbo. I turned out the lights, leaving the scenes on the dining room walls to disappear in darkness.

When I joined Mother in the living room that next afternoon I saw her photograph albums piled on the living room sofa; just as she had been sorting through table linens and unused porcelain mementos to give away to her children, she had been sifting through her memories, choosing moments to give me for safekeeping. As we talked, the afternoon sun filtered through the closed drapes on either side of her chair. In the South even in winter, people keep their houses dark; blinds and drapes remain closed. Perhaps the reason is to protect the furniture from the burning rays of the southern sun, or perhaps it is merely habit—a vestige lingering from days before screens and air conditioning. I always want to open them, to have the warmth and light, but they remained closed today as we sat together, Mother in her recliner and I close to her in the Chippendale wing chair Mother and Daddy bought in Charleston on their honeymoon. That chair, the television set, and my grandmother's French tulip-wood desk surround the great brown mechanical chair in which Mother spends her afternoons, reclined and motionless, gazing with unseeing eyes at the room crowded with books, Oriental rugs, and antiques: standing out among them the English plate table with a Staffordshire lamp, the butler's tray coffee table with crystal decanter, a needlepoint footstool, several comfortable chairs, and mahogany tables laden with objects. Over on the wide window ledge sits the torso of a woman, carved by Enrique Alferez, a sculptor friend of Daddy's. Mother told me he carried the large piece of wood on his back all the way from Mexico to New Orleans so that he could carve it for them as a gift to my father for helping him during difficult times.

Mother's new monstrous lounge chair dominates half of the living room these days, easing her to her feet when she needs to rise. It stands near the corner where the baby grand piano once stood. I can remember hiding under that piano when the doctor came to give us typhoid shots. I never knew until I was grown the significance of those shots; I only knew how much they hurt. But the urgency to immunize us—my sister, brother, and me—is part of the story, one of the dark secrets that Daddy and Mother kept hidden; like the alligator gars under the river, they never surfaced, not until the day my father died.

My sister, brother, and I were home when Daddy died. It was spring vacation, and I had come home from Connecticut College with Alby to celebrate our engagement. Daddy died the day after our party. He died on April Fool's Day, with a drink in his hand, waiting for my mother to finish dressing for dinner with my uncles and aunt at my grandparents' home on Audubon Place. I don't remember much about the funeral except that Mother did not want us to look at Daddy in his coffin. I don't even re-member if any of my friends were there.

After the funeral, alone with me in the room we shared as children, my sister sat on her bed reading Daddy's will. I was sitting by the window envying the rain drops dancing on the window ledge, wondering how I could leave to go back East again. I could not envision summoning up enough energy to study for comprehensives; then, if I passed them, would I feel any pleasure in celebrating the end of college and my own wedding? Would I ever feel ebullient again? The rain, the closed windows, and the gray walls answered that I would not. Suddenly Betty uttered a shrill "My God!" and jumped up, the papers rustling in her hand.

"What . . . what?" I asked.

In a voice very close to hysterics she read the legal language that stated that Daddy had been married before—our Daddy—to someone else before our mother. I remember my sister's shocked laugh at this discovery kept hidden all those years and her reading that passage several times to me. I simply stared back at her in disbelief—as if she and I were acting roles in a play I had not rehearsed, and I had forgotten my lines. After a moment of silence, we bolted down the hall to Mother's room. Almost as if she did not know the answer, Mother had to have it posed to her several times, prompted like an actress who forgot her lines, before she slowly unfolded a sketchy version of Daddy's painful story about losing a wife and a baby as a result of typhoid fever. She tried to explain to us that sorrow and fear had caused them to bury this story, believing that it would not surface; she claimed that there never had seemed an appropriate time to tell us. I know now that they wanted to forget, to deny that terrible tragedy by building a new marriage and beginning a new family. Had she indeed forgotten?

After Mother revealed the truth she and Daddy had kept from us, this new knowledge for a time strangely dissipated the grief we were feeling, but I struggled to deal with my loss as I turned again to my affairs. Although at times sorrow overwhelmed me, I managed to finish college, shift into marriage, and move permanently to Connecticut. Distance perhaps added to Mother's reluctance to talk about Daddy's past, but she never filled in the details of the story. It remained a topic sentence without a paragraph until years later, when I was able to fit the piece about the typhoid shots and Mother's obsessive fear of germs into the fabric of my life, weaving it together with the story of my dead half-brother and his young mother, Daddy's first family who were born to me that day my father died. I wasn't told their names; unlike the places my father named, the trees and the ponds, these people were denied their permanence; they were meant to be forgotten.

As we sat that afternoon in the living room, the sun shot a ray of warmth through the open part of the drapes, sparrows sang in the crape myrtles outside the open window, and Mother began without prompting. In a strong voice and in language that sounded rehearsed, she revealed the story that I never had heard detailed before, about my father, his other family, and her courtship and marriage. "The great theme of my life," she told me, "has been my love for my husband, which started in my teens, and was fraught with so much difficulty because there was so much objection, first from my parents, who thought about his past life and what had happened to him." In one long, uninterrupted voice she narrated the story that I had waited for thirty-nine years to hear.

I
Caroline's Story

1

The Summer of 1927

*M*other was taken away by her parents, Felix and Julia, to spend the summer of 1927 in Charlevoix, Michigan, away from the tropical heat of the city and away from the passion that had flamed between her and Daddy for seven years. Even though she was twenty-eight, her family still believed they could extinguish that flame. A previous summer they had whisked her off to Europe, hoping that museums, cathedrals, and spas would cultivate new desires and bring her to her senses. Now they aimed to cool her affection by resort frivolity: swimming in Lake Michigan, playing tennis, riding horseback, and dancing the Charleston with amiable young men at the Charlevoix Beach Hotel. They knew that this resort attracted the proper Jewish families from places like Cincinnati, and they wanted her to make the correct selection.

Instead of the distance pulling Caroline and Leon apart, it drew them closer; their love deepened and their letters expressed in heightened prose the intimacy forbidden them. They wrote every day. Even on Sunday, Caroline's letters were brought to Leon's New Orleans apartment special delivery by a mailman on motorcycle who blew a whistle to announce his presence.

Even though Charlevoix pleasures reminded her of her girlhood, summer-camp days of freedom from school and routines, Caroline agonized over Leon's plight—struggling to establish his practice while dealing with his partner Julius' increasing irritability and inactivity. Leon and Caroline hoped to change her family's negative opinion. She wanted her father to approve of Leon and agree to their plans to marry, but proving himself while apart from her seemed a lonely quest for both of them. Caroline thought it strange that once they knew of her love, her father and brother Julius found faults in Leon that never before had been issues. She watched their previous admiration for Leon's spirit and talent dissolve into doubt and disdain. They objected to his age; they questioned his past experiences with women; and they worried about his ability to make money as an architect.

Although they never mentioned it, Caroline wondered if Leon's family background might be an issue. She knew a little about his family and realized that her parents could be concerned that the German and French Jewish community might consider Leon's background unacceptable. Although Leon's father came from Alsace, he was a first-generation American—a newcomer, which ranked him lower than people with greater longevity in the community. Then, too, some time after arriving as a new immigrant, Theodore Weiss fell on hard times. He worked as a merchant for a firm in Baltimore, but he and his partner found themselves bankrupt. Although Theodore worked hard to recover his losses and paid off all the debts, Caroline wondered if Felix could possibly believe that Leon's father's misfortune could cause Leon's character to be flawed.

She knew that in the eyes of the community, Leon's maternal grandparents would be ranked as immigrants because they were born in Eastern Europe. They had emigrated from Poland, so Leon might be considered unsuitable by the established Jewish New Orleanians. Then, too, Lena and all her siblings were raised in an orphanage when their mother died of yellow fever and their father lost his money and also died. After the death of his wife, Sarah, Lazarus Silverstein, in an attempt to escape the epidemic, had taken the children to St. Francisville and had entrusted all the stock and capital from his jewelry store to a man he thought was his friend. After Lazarus contracted yellow fever and died, the family could not regain ownership of his store, since the man apparently disappeared with the money. Unfortunately, that meant the children were dispatched to the Jewish Children's Home, known then as the Jewish Home for Orphans. Caroline wondered if Lena's impoverished, homeless origins could be another strike against Leon.

Knowing her father's position in the community and his desire to maintain his respectability, she suspected that Leon's ancestry and not his character was the cause of Felix's objections. She wondered if Felix could possibly fear he'd be slighted by the community if his daughter married a man whose maternal grandparents were "ethnic" Jews. She knew that when the first wave of eastern Orthodox Jews arrived in the city, the already integrated Reform Jews, now second generation, felt threatened: believing themselves French or German Americans and not Jewish Americans, they worried that their social acceptability might be undermined by these new arrivals, whose dress and behavior blatantly identified them as Jews. That was long ago, she reasoned. But then again, proper background was valued in this community that still worshiped aristocracy.

In business matters, Felix always acted with generosity and fairness. He willingly gave legal and business advice to Russian clients, but since he and others of French and German descent moved comfortably in the city's social and business circles, they distanced themselves from these unassimilated Eastern European Jews. Some New Orleans Jews even labeled the poor among these newcomers as professional paupers—"Jewish tramps" who did not deserve charity.

Caroline knew that, even though they didn't actually admit it, her parents looked down upon people with Polish connections; but, she wondered, would they reject Leon for having a Polish ancestor? Good grief, she thought. Lena's Polish parents were no longer around to embarrass anyone. They had died so long ago—about the 1860s, she thought. Even if they were alive, in light of her father's dedication to reform movements in politics and to charity in civic affairs, she wondered whether he would be judgmental of Leon's grandmother's place of birth. After all, Lena had been born in Louisiana and had married an Alsatian Jew. Would they object to Leon's father having been a naturalized citizen—first generation—even though he made enough money now to live reasonably well? Wouldn't the family now be considered respectable—and acceptable? Although she knew the old prejudices were not buried, would they arise and cause Felix to believe that Leon wasn't the right choice for her? It was all so complex and irrational. She couldn't believe that all this mattered.

Leon had awakened an ardor in Caroline that could not be cooled even in this Eden of green lawns, gooseberry hedges, and rose gardens. She felt for him a physical love that grew stronger; she missed him intensely, particularly when collecting wildflowers or marveling at shapes of clouds or tree branches against the cool blue of the Michigan sky. Leon's passion for natural wonders and his poetic spirit pulled her to him. For his part, despite the solitude and emptiness of the city without her, he found solace in writing and reward in seeing the paper visions of his plans and his drawings grow into cement and steel structures.

The high point of the summer for him was the completion of the Eola Hotel in Natchez and his journey there to participate in the opening celebrations. Caroline received several letters written during his visit that expressed his exultation and pride in hearing everyone praise him for being the creator of this beautiful modern building: its iron balconies and portico blended in with downtown Natchez, yet the structure incorporated all of the latest innovations in hotel design and equipment. People connected with the city and the hotel applauded him for the engineering accomplishments, the artistic design of the building, and the decor of the rooms. When the city officials gathered in the Audubon Room, with its floor-to-ceiling reproductions of Audubon's Mississippi bird prints, they toasted his fine taste and careful selection of details. Leon enjoyed being the center of attention, and since Caroline had helped choose the prints for the Audubon Room and the murals with plantation life motifs for the Mississippi River meeting room, she felt happy that their first project together, their shared creation, had received so many compliments. His letters also expressed sorrow that she could not be there for the occasion. The completion of this building and the praise he received for it gave him the energy and the spirit to return to his hectic office to ready the plans for bids on the Pontchartrain and Jung Hotels.

All that summer he spent long hours at his drafting table or negotiating specifications with contractors; but late in the evening, under the ceiling fan in his apartment, he devoted himself to writing letters and poems to Caroline. Writing and building were for him similar processes, both springing from the imagination and urged onward by creative energy to emerge as finished structures. He ended one letter by writing that "while steel on steel and stone on stone, the busy workers upward build our hopes, we rest, my Darling, from our labors and our pains,—my head upon your lap, my eyes to yours, your smile to mine—a dream of perfect love and peace . . . that joy, to think about!"

As he worked all that summer, Caroline played the role of dutiful daughter to father Felix and mother Julia, keeping herself from gloom by anticipating daily letters and the end of summer.

The June day that they arrived in Charlevoix was too cloudy and cool for the beach, but Caroline strolled down to Lake Michigan anyhow. She was still dressed in her traveling suit, since the steamer trunks had not yet been delivered from the railroad station. Wanting to be alone and fearing her cousin Helen or her sister, Ruth, would follow her, she tore off her shoes and raced through the opening in the gooseberry hedge and across the lawn in her stocking feet. Winding her way through the grove of cherry trees, she reached the edge of the water, spread her shawl on the grass, and sat and watched a sailboat dipping and pitching far out on the lake. She wondered how she would endure being held hostage here, listening to her father's objections and having the family pummel her with ugly accusations about Leon. She hated having left him alone, especially after they had finally made a commitment to each other. Leon had been through so many years of loneliness after the loss of his first family. She worried how in the world she could find a way to convince her father to listen to her and believe in her judgment about Leon; perhaps he'd at least accept the fact that they loved each other. Caroline did not want to spend the summer like Penelope, avoiding eligible suitors while Leon sailed alone fighting giants.

She thought about the seven years of contention and uncertainty that they had already fumbled through, and she felt oppressed in spite of the brisk breeze that blew in from the lake. She tucked her feet under her skirt and dug in her bag for the letter she had found placed on her pillow by some romantic hotel maid. She opened the letter and listened to herself read again Leon's description of their romance. She loved the way he wrote and wished she could write as eloquently. Her letters seemed so plain they embarrassed her, even though Leon had said how beautiful they were. As she read this letter she thought that the phrases sounded like the chapter titles of a nineteenth-century novel, like her favorite George Eliot novel, *Middlemarch*. She delighted in his poetic phrases as she heard him declare: "My Darling Caroline. . . ." He was right. They had experienced, as he phrased it, "all the emotions and the sentiments; all the sorrows and the joys; all the blasted hopes and happy plans; all the obstacles, objections, doubts and fears; the near-parting of the ways; the intervention of the confidante; the climacteric meeting on the breakwater by the lake in the moonlight; the saving grace of a sense of humor; the inquisitions; the pledge."

Yes, she thought, their love had traveled through what he had called "the gamut of human feelings," but Caroline and Leon believed that now, at last, they had finally arrived at a peaceful shore: they were certain of each other. That was "the pledge" that they had made to each other. All they needed now was to convince the others so that they could become officially engaged and shout it to all the world.

She could still taste the bitterness of her father's words last fall, forbidding her to see Leon again. "He is not an honorable man. I have it from reliable authority that he . . . his reputation is bad. I will not go into detail. Just hear me. He is too old for you. He will not make a good husband. He's been married. He failed at that, and I have heard he doesn't work hard. He will never amount to much. . . . Caroline, you must break with him for your own sake." He had turned to his docile wife for assistance and, in a voice sweetened with honey, had closed the discussion by saying, "Dear Julia, please tell Caroline that we want her to be happy. Leon will not make her happy."

After speaking to Julia, her father turned back to Caroline. The proclamation that followed, offered like a litany, rapidly and without emotion, sounded as if it came from a Sunday radio preacher, and as she listened to her parents, her knees felt weak. She had looked to her mother as a source of support before her father's last declaration, but when Caroline saw those thin lips tighten, she knew defeat. "All right," she remembered saying. "I'll try not seeing him." She had left the room, fighting back tears she refused to release. After that ultimatum, Leon's name had not been mentioned by anyone in the family. Once Leon agreed to the separation, Caroline spent the next five months in a dizzy world of dances and dates with other men. She liked some of them, she acknowledged, but none had the excitement of Leon.

In spite of the promise to her father, on several occasions she went to dinner at Leon's apartment during the winter of their separation; but since Leon's father dined with them, Caroline and Leon didn't feel they were transgressing. At dinner they spoke awkwardly of events, avoiding anything personal, discussing Leon's latest designs, the weather, Mr. Weiss's health, or unusual psychological test results Caroline encountered when she had worked in a clinic. Interviewing shell-shocked soldiers had brought the devastating effects of the war close to her, and she still remembered the stories young men had told her—even years later. When she sat across from these soldiers and listened, trying to untangle the meaning of their experiences in the trenches, she imagined being there herself; she knew she couldn't have told such horrible stories with the grim humor these men displayed. Talking to Leon and his father helped her sort out her own recollections.

These subjects were as close as the two of them could get to intimacy; no ardent words passed between them, nor did they have any physical contact. It was strange having been so recently entangled and now having become unwound into such separate threads. Though the dinners were not the clandestine romantic affairs they wanted them to be, Caroline had climbed the back stairs of the building to avoid gossip and to prevent evidence from reaching Jackson Avenue that they had been seeing each another surreptitiously. They laughed when, one afternoon, she arrived with the ice man. They seriously wished they could be real lovers, dining alone by candlelight instead of acting like formal acquaintances under the eyes of a chaperon.

Thank goodness this pretense had ended when Leon's cousin Stella assumed the role of confidante. Like Juliet's nurse, she had intervened—or interfered. That happened when Caroline visited her in Hackensack, New Jersey, in March. Caroline was finishing her first year studying psychology in graduate school at Bryn Mawr and had taken the train up to New York and out to New Jersey after class one Friday morning. She was going to meet friends in the city and then planned to spend the afternoon with Cousin Stella.

Caroline had never met any of Leon's aunts or uncles—they had died many years before she met Leon—but he had told her about his aunt, Carrie Silverstein Stern, Stella's mother, and about Stella's talented sister, Lillian Bret Harte, who was now living in California and working on a collection of poems, later published as *A Handful of Stars*. Caroline liked to hear about Leon's family and hoped one day to meet Lillian, an accomplished poet and photographer. She would love to talk to her about Bret Harte, the grandfather of Lillian's husband and also hear about Lillian's great friend and admirer Isadora Duncan. Caroline loved being around creative people, especially women who seemed to live and express life so freely.

She knew Stella was Leon's favorite cousin, and soon she found out why. Sitting in Stella's living room in her brownstone home, Caroline felt comfortable and relaxed. Stella was one of those people who knew how to talk with young people; she had a way of listening, and Caroline rattled on about her studies, her friends, books, and especially the children's book Stella was writing. It intrigued her that Stella published her books under the name Stella George Perry, attaching her given name in front of her husband's full name as did her sister, Lillian Bret Harte.

Ever since graduating from Barnard, Stella had been writing. The voice she used in her books, that narrative, reflective, somewhat moralistic voice, spoke out to Caroline this afternoon as the conversation turned to Leon. Caroline found herself confiding in Stella as they talked about her frustrations and Leon's tragedy. She heard herself confess to Stella her fear of making a decision, not only because of her parents' objections but also because of her own intense uncertainty about marriage. She had been so protected that, at her age, she was still naïve and inexperienced. "They just won't let me go. I feel so torn sometimes. . . . I'm afraid—I mean, how do you know it's right? They won't talk to me. . . . Did you—I mean, how did you know?"

Stella smiled at her warmly and answered, "My dear, you know. And you are the only one to listen to. Listen inside . . . to your own voice within. Believe it. Then make up your mind and stick to it. Follow your feelings . . . give in to them. It's all right if you feel it's right . . . and then, it'll be a good marriage."

Caroline was surprised by the ease with which they became intimate: she had not talked about these things even with her sister or with friends. There was something special about this woman. Perhaps that's why Leon's nieces and nephews wrote letters to her with the salutation "Dear Cousin Stella Dear." Caroline remembered she had laughed to hear that everyone addressed Stella that way.

As the afternoon slipped by, they settled down with their tea and talked and talked about Leon. Then, after they had eaten the last of the cakes, Stella got up from her chair and walked over to the window. Slowly, without turning, she spoke in a soft but firm voice, as if to the bare rose bushes outside, that time was up for this courting stage, that Caroline should marry Leon or let him go. "Look," she said. "I believe that you two are in love. I think that it is a great love, but you cannot keep Leon waiting any longer. It's too difficult for him. Marry him soon," she urged, "or give him up."

Except for the ticking of the grandfather clock in the hall, there was silence in the room for a long while. The words "Give him up" echoed in that silence. At first they stung Caroline, but after a bit she felt a twinge of relief seep through her. It was as if someone had given her permission to sign her own checks. She thought it strange that she had to have someone else give it to her, but at last she had the authority to make a decision. She wondered if other women took as long to decide about marrying, if parents always made it difficult. How she would lift their prohibitions, she did not know, but now she at least believed she had the power to act. She looked at the empty teapot and rose to leave. As she gathered up her coat and purse, she turned to the small woman in the tattered shawl who stood at the door. Caroline's coat and bag fell to the floor as she moved to throw her arms around Stella. "There, there," Stella said. "It will be all right." Taking both of Caroline's hands in her own, Stella drew her closer and kissed her forehead.

Caroline picked up her things and tried to speak in a decisive voice. "I promise . . . I'll let you know. I'll make my decision this summer. I will. Goodbye . . . and . . . well, thank you."

That day marked for her the end of her indecision. She had tried separation enough times before to know that she couldn't give up Leon. That wasn't the answer. That winter snowstorm of social life, drifting from party to party, had not cooled her desire to be with him. She spent weekends with the Baton Rouge gang, especially Si Mendelsohn, and she visited Cincinnati relatives who introduced her to necking parties and to Bud Brown. She really liked him and he became her Cincinnati beau. Of all her many suitors, however, Julian Sacks in his suit and vest seemed ready-made to please her parents. She tried to fall for him. They went to the theater, to museums, and out dancing. They dined together at late-night suppers, discussing art and literature, and ended the evenings in the quiet of her parlor watching the glow from the coal-burning stove. She enjoyed these evenings and even his kisses, but she did not want to marry him or any of the others. Not after meeting Leon. For from the first moment she saw him, she knew, in spite of the cliché, that it had been love at first sight.

The day she first saw Leon had been an unusually warm March afternoon. She had been sitting on the porch of her house on Jackson Avenue watching a mockingbird in the sweet-olive tree, the tree that her father had moved from his father's home on Esplanade Avenue. She was thinking of the meaning of that tradition in New Orleans of planting a sweet-olive tree in the garden when a new home was completed, and how she adored the almond odor that drifted in from the tree on the warm spring breeze. She watched the mockingbird fly up to a taller tree as she heard the streetcar rattle to a stop. It was then that she saw a man dressed in a linen suit, starched collar and tie, step down from it into her life.

Her brother Julius had invited Leon to their house for Sunday dinner, a family ritual everyone was expected to attend. Julius and Leon had become partners and close friends since the early twenties and often dined together at Kolb's, Leon's favorite downtown restaurant; but this Sunday was the first family meal Leon had been invited to. He had met Julius' sister Ruth, brother George, and mother and father, but had not met Caroline. All during the courses and conversation, she found him staring at her each time she looked up from her plate. She could barely follow the discussion, even though ideas about architecture and vivid descriptions of buildings usually held her attention during family meals. After the ice cream and demitasse, Felix excused himself, as he was accustomed to listening to opera on the radio after dinner. Julius and Leon remained at the table, with Caroline still frozen to her seat, even though she always hated long sessions at Sunday dinner and was often teased for finding excuses to get away. Subsequent Sunday dinners with Leon present at the table led to afternoon walks around the garden and talks under the arbor near the lily pond in the garden. That was how it began.

She thought back over their story as she sat by the lake in Michigan wishing the summer away. The air was becoming more uncomfortable as the sky turned even grayer. She looked at the darkening lake and thought about another lake, Lake Pontchartrain, that last night with Leon before she left for Michigan. That lake had been dark that night too, but she remembered the moon that had lit the ripples and brightened the cloudless night. They had planned how the night would be theirs. The steamer trunks had been packed and shipped earlier in the week, and she had only some last-minute items to fold and pack in her train case. She had finished placing her nightgown and robe in the top compartment just as he arrived.

They had sat for a while on the front porch, but feeling the need to be off by themselves, she bid her parents good-night, promised she would not stay out late, and climbed into the car next to him. After a quiet drive out to the lake they walked along the seawall out onto the breakwater, away from the lights of the pavilion and the passing cars. Out there under the stars, watching the lights of the distant fishing boats and listening to the ebb of the waves, she whispered, "Leon, no one else will do. I can't stand those others. I love you and I must have only you."

The sound of the wind and the waves and her voice rippled through him and he held her close. His only answer, a gasp, sounded more like a cry. Then a quiet, "My darling . . . my dearest Caroline . . . we will be together."

"Leon, promise me you will keep our secret. I will marry you at the end of summer. In September . . . I promise." The water lapped at the rocks in rhythm with their heartbeats. The words "I promise" echoed strangely in her ear until she recalled having voiced them to Cousin Stella a few months before.

She felt the agony of the summer's separation but assured him she would spend the summer in Michigan battling to change her parents' opinion. "I'll make them understand. This summer will be our last separation. I swear."

The letter in her hand spoke of that night and the pledge they had made to each other. It also acknowledged that barriers still existed but that their deep love "would weather the gales of doubts and fears" through the long summer months. Taking one last look at the deepening shadows and the white lawn chairs turning blue in the twilight, Caroline stared again at his words: "I caress you in my thoughts—between sentences and paragraphs. I live the evening with you in spirit." Slowly she folded the letter, tucked it into her bag, and strolled back to the cottage to unpack her trunk and settle in for the long summer months of waiting.

One chapter of their book seemed to have closed, for at long last she felt relief at having made up her mind. But there remained for both of them the great task of peeling off the layers of doubt and the misjudgments that others had cast upon Leon. It seemed incongruous that her brother Julius, since he was Leon's partner and friend, would hit the hardest. Ironically, instead of harmonizing with him in designing and building, as he used to, Julius generated an atmosphere of discord in the office. Not only was he irritable and uncooperative, all summer long he devised new guerrilla tactics.

Even though Leon joked in his letters to her about being called "shiftless and disinterested," he had to contend daily with Julius' abuse and even indifference toward the projects the office was handling. Julius' hostility and his absence from the office some afternoons when he was off playing golf doubled the pressures on Leon.

And Julius, he thought, had been a friend. Not too many years before, they had shared some wild evenings together in Uncle Jules's French Quarter studio. It had been Uncle Jules, Julius' uncle, who had introduced them after Leon had designed some buildings for him. All three men had been bachelors then. Now Jules lived in a proper home on St. Charles Avenue following his marriage to Beulah, a fun-loving woman from Natchez who had a pet parrot she taught to curse. "You're a son of a bitch," the parrot would repeat. Perhaps, Leon had conjectured, the parrot only echoed Beulah's mutterings about her husband, whom she had been unable to tame. Leon wondered how Julius could be so judgmental now. Yes, Julius had married Vera and had settled down, but in former days he had participated freely with Leon and Jules in the bohemian life they led in the French Quarter and the raucous weekend house parties at Jules's fishing camp in Little Woods. It was maddening.

On several occasions Leon tried to talk to Julius and to George, Caroline's older brother, but the only response was silence. In the days following one of these encounters, Julius hardly spoke to him: they greeted one another politely in the morning and spoke formally about their work. Then Julius began acting more aggressively vengeful: he demanded more of the draftsman's time for himself, missed appointments, and endlessly complained: about his back, about Leon's unorthodox working hours, or about the way Leon handled matters. He refused to work on the Barnett furniture store, an art deco building on the corner of Carondelet and Lafayette streets, expressing his belief that because of Leon's poor judgment the office would lose money on it. His complaints were aired in the office and long distance to his father, but the bids for the Barnett building came in, proving that Leon's judgment had been correct. He wrote to Caroline, "Julius paid me the Barnett bet which he lost. I am inclosing the check to you in evidence. Isn't it pretty—and meaningful?—one of the tails of the dragon." Caroline was glad that Leon's letters to her showed a touch of irony about his situation and that he didn't seem bitter or in any way jealous that her summer was full of play and his so stressful.

Many nights Leon dined at Kolb's, having his favorite German meal of sauerbraten, potato pancakes, and a draft of dark beer, served at his special table by his regular waiter. Kolb's, a downtown restaurant on St. Charles Street in the commercial district, half a block from Canal Street, looked on the outside like a typical French Quarter building with iron grillwork on the balcony. But inside, the Old World atmosphere of exposed dark wood rafters and marble floors and table tops marked it as distinctively German. Its most unusual feature was the ceiling fans connected by belts to one motor. They hung low on chains from the rafters. It was a decidedly male establishment. After dinner Leon returned to his office and worked alone until midnight.

If his letters had not revealed his enthusiasm and creative energy, his working so hard might have seemed motivated only by the desire to win the approval of Caroline's parents or to pierce holes in Julius' charges. In any case, he devoted his time to his profession and his thoughts to Caroline.

One particularly muggy evening, he sipped a cold glass of bourbon and soda and wished for an end to the "exile." He took up the writing portfolio she had given him and wrote about an imagined "dream of perfect love and peace . . . in a beautiful spot somewhere, like your arbor by the lily pool—where a gently sloping knoll, velvet-grassy covered, dips its sandy margins into the cool refreshing waters of a mirror-lake; where sweetly-scented trees stand as sheltering barriers from the sun; where all is peace and quiet, love and harmony. There I see you, Dearest, seated in the checquered shade." He had left that letter unfinished, had gone out into the still air and walked a few blocks up St. Charles. But when he found that it was too hot for even a stroll, he returned and tried unsuccessfully to sleep. The heat, the frustration, and the loneliness oppressed him.

Caroline haunted the lobby of the hotel each morning after breakfast, waiting for the mail to arrive with her special letter. When it did, she found a quiet table on the terrace near her favorite yellow rosebush and devoured his tender phrases of love for her. His letters praised her for her sensibility and intelligence, especially in response to some of her moments of self-doubt. When she called herself "silly," complained that her letters were "long ones with little news," or referred to herself as "dumb Dora Caroline" with a "wishy-washy mind," he wrote back complimenting her for a "splendidly descriptive" letter painting the scenes of Charlevoix so vividly, especially the "lady slippers, and daisies" along the roadsides; he told her how well she expressed her "sweetly affectionate" thoughts to him. As she looked away from the page, she tried to hear the voice that wrote, "No dream has measured even part of the sun-kissed heights to which your devotion has exalted me."

As she read the paragraphs describing his work, she tried to imagine the buildings that Leon shaped on the drawing board. She followed along in her mind as he described in detail the process by which he prepared blueprints and specifications for the Jung Hotel. These specifications were "huge documents," requiring detailed outlines of "wiring, ventilating, refrigeration, kitchen equipment, structural steel and concrete, and plumbing and fuel oil systems." The specifications had to be checked and edited before being bound and ready for drafting. To expedite the procedure for drafting the final plans, Leon explained, he had developed a new process of drawing "small scale working plans . . . complete studies on a small scale" from which the working drawings could be made.

Her belief in him deepened as she read the letters describing his work. As she read she began to appreciate his intelligence, his skill, and his artistic genius. She memorized the words in his last letter that reassured her that, despite the fatigue he felt after a long, challenging day of work, "writing to you is no effort. It is just drifting with the tide of my thoughts, snatching an idea here, another there, like picking flowers from the passing banks of the stream, arranging them into the semblance of order, tying them together, and sending the bunch to you."

One evening in July, Caroline came back from horseback riding with Helen and some of her other friends and thought she'd take a short swim before dinner. As she opened the screen door to the cottage, her father handed her a letter. She could tell right away that it was from Julius. It had obviously been read but was neatly folded and placed in the envelope he had addressed to his father. Her mother, sitting over by the window sewing her grandchild Carol's pinafore, did not look up from her work. After handing Caroline the letter, her father returned to his rocking chair, where he had been looking over legal papers that had arrived in the same packet of letters. He watched her face as she read the letter Julius had written. It began with Julius apologizing for having to play the role of informer but then went on to say that someone had told him something about Leon that Julius thought his father should know. He wrote that Leon once had kept a mistress named Juanita, obviously a woman of questionable character— someone with that name surely was low class, Julius argued. The letter went on to say that apparently there were other women as well. As she read his letter, Caroline felt outraged and betrayed by her brother. It seemed that his goal was to break up her relationship even if it meant sullying his partner's reputation by unloading a Pandora's box of ugly notions for his father to wallow in. Caroline wondered if his cruelty arose from jealousy of Leon's talent or from a desire to score points with his father. She handed back the letter and asked to be excused for a few minutes—to bathe and dress, she said.

She lingered a while in her room trying to locate the inner strength she had so newly discovered in herself since her visit to Stella dear. There was really nothing in the letter that she and Leon had not discussed. She knew that after the death of his first wife and son, he had tried to heal his wounds in ways that he later regretted. She had needed time to understand and forgive him. Then after some reflection, she had removed her last doubts by concluding that Leon's affair was only natural for an artistic man of passionate nature. She did not consider his behavior promiscuous or scandalous, as Julius had labeled it. Caroline pitied Leon for his loss, but mostly she admired him for having the courage to love someone once again.

She remembered the day he had told her about little Teddy's death from typhoid fever. There were no tears as he described the child's torturous dying, but his voice weakened as he came to the end of the story—the last terrible days of high fever, vomiting, diarrhea, and acute pain—when the six-year-old body weakened and wore out from the massive infection. The coma following the final convulsion almost seemed a relief. Caroline could feel Leon's agony as he relived the death and then the desperate struggle to console his wife as she, hysterical, threatened suicide. Urgently he had begged her not to take her life. He tried to hold her back, but she was too distraught and determined. Caroline remembered that the lines in Leon's face deepened and his mouth quivered when he whispered the word *poison* to explain his wife's cruel death. The night before she took her life, she pleaded with him to join her. She wanted both of them to follow their baby to death. Caroline had shuddered when he told her his harrowing choice: like Orpheus, to follow his wife to the underworld, or to stay behind in the living world without her. Fortunately, what kept him in the world of the living, he told Caroline, was his love for his parents and unwillingness to hurt them. Once she learned the grim story and reflected upon it, Caroline decided that the love she and Leon shared would assuage his pain. She believed that courage and the power of love could obliterate all the troubles of the past. She wanted above anything else to make him happy.

She would prove all of her father's objections to her marrying Leon unfounded. She would spoil her father's assertion that a man with such a tragic past would not have the stability to be a dependable husband, and she would defend Leon against Julius' charges. She did not believe, as they did, in that old myth that Leon was culpable, that he in some way failed and was responsible for his wife's suicide—or that her death presaged un-happiness for Caroline as his second wife. And she trusted him completely.

After a hasty bath, Caroline selected Leon's favorite yellow linen dress from her closet, pulled it over her head, brushed her hair so that no loose curls fell on her face, and carefully applied a bit of rouge to her cheeks. She took one last look at the image of herself in the mirror and fixed a deter-mined expression on her face to carry back to the sitting room. Before leaving her bedroom, she glanced over to her writing table, as if to reassure herself that Leon's photograph still stood there, the one of him in his army uniform: khaki knickers, high boots, and jaunty wide-brimmed hat. She loved the way he stood with his hands on his hips as if to challenge the world. Yet he would not confront her father. Instead he stood aside, prom-ising Caroline's father another summer away—for Caroline to be free to make her decision without coercion. Leon believed her parents would be fair. She thought with bitterness of Leon's letter to her, promising to keep faith with her father "for the sake of the honor of our perfect love."

When she returned, she started to tell her father that she believed her brother's tales were specious—that Julius had no business interfering; but before she could finish her charge, her father was ready with an ultimatum. He would place an immediate injunction on their relationship until Leon provided medical evidence that he was free of disease. He went on to inform her that Leon's past behavior and the fact that he was forty-five probably meant that he could not give her children, so that for her own happiness, she should find someone else. With that he gathered up his papers, said, "Come, Julia," and they both left the room.

Caroline stood motionless until she heard the screen door of the cottage close behind them. Alone in the sitting room, she gave in to the tears that she had held back so resolutely. Suddenly, she saw over in the corner of the room the empty steamer trunks standing like sentinels waiting to be summoned. How she wished she had the strength to leave. What kept her here? Whose promise should she honor, hers to Leon or his to her father?

Caroline touched the top of her trunk, stood a moment in silence, and then flew to her room and pulled open the drawer of her writing table. She would write and tell him she was going to come home. On top of a pile of letters was the one she had received from him that morning. When she looked at the date of the letter, she realized that it was probably written on the same day Julius had composed his deadly missive. Leon's letter alluded to the problem of Julius' attitude about the office, which had seemed to intensify with the August heat, but the letter ended on a positive note. She skimmed the first two pages and then read the rest of his letter slowly, as if to commit it to memory, for she loved his spirit, especially his confidence in himself. She heard his strong voice assert: "My very soul is in my efforts. Something within me sees the Truth. I know I am right. . . . It is not the judgment of my finite mind, my Darling. There is a spiritual force guiding me—I have faith in this. I am honest and zealous, deeply serious; and no obstacles can block the way of my spirit. . . . If this beautiful optimism is a fault, and makes me stand alone, an outcast; then my Precious Sweetheart, like the pharisees, I do indeed 'thank God that I am not like other men.' . . . I can not let mercenary motives, miserliness, the lure of gold, the appraisal of my fellow-men as so many means to the end of my own enrichment, kill my free spirit, rob me of my higher impulses, and make me love the things of the flesh more than the things of the spirit!"

Indeed, Caroline thought, Leon is not like other men. Thank God. He has an intensity, a spirituality, that draws me to him. I need to be near him to hear his words. They infuse me with energy and enlightenment. I want excitement in my life, and even if we can't have a family, I will have him. He is all that I need and desire. I will pack and leave tonight. Caroline took out a piece of stationery and began to write. She wrote about half a page and then stopped abruptly: the obedient child in her told her she should wait until morning. Slowly she placed Leon's letter and the page she had written to him back in the drawer, closed it, and left the room to join her parents at dinner.

Being a woman of the twenties, accustomed to obeying a father's authority, Caroline spent the next few days agonizing. She wished she could settle the matter by catching the next Pullman home, but her family had succeeded in planting fears. She wanted to listen to her heart, but she had never been one to act rashly, preferring instead to seek answers and act rationally. She had finished the letter and had mailed it special delivery, telling Leon what had happened—about Julius' latest offensive and her father's latest ultimatum, but she said nothing about returning to New Orleans.

Since she had to wait almost a week for his response, Caroline tried to keep busy taking long hikes with her cousin Helen and reading her favorite Elizabeth Barrett Browning sonnets down at the lake; but the agony of indecision overwhelmed her and she desperately wanted someone to talk to. She certainly couldn't talk to Julius' wife, Vera, who once said a girl should not kiss until she became engaged; Caroline had responded that she wouldn't get engaged before kissing. Maybe Mother, she thought.

Her old store of fear and indecision crowded in on her, interfering with her sleep and occupying her consciousness during the day. What if the others are right? Maybe marrying an older man is a mistake. Finally, one afternoon she joined her mother in the main lounge of the hotel. They sat on two large wicker chairs, ordered tea, and smiled uncomfortably at each another. As Caroline tried to form her question, she remembered the only other time she had tried to ask about sex. Her mother had told her then about menstruation but also warned that kissing a man made a girl pregnant; Caroline had believed her for a number of years. Oh, well, she thought, I'll try again. Carefully she placed her cup of tea back in its saucer and in a quiet voice told her mother how much she loved Leon and that she wanted to marry him. "Mother," she said, trying to hold her voice steady. "Tell me, what has Leon's age to do with not being able to have babies?"

Her mother blushed the color of the rose in the bud vase on the tea table and, as she put down her cup, spilled a drop of tea on the white damask tablecloth. "Caroline," she said uncertainly, "you must not ask me these questions. I—I don't know . . . I don't know how to talk about . . . these things. You have to ask Father." She signaled the waiter for the check, dabbed with her napkin at the tea spot on the cloth, and stood up to leave.

On a walk to town to buy some cherries for their picnic the next afternoon, Caroline poured out her misery to her cousin Helen. Leaving out most of the particulars, Caroline only told Helen that her parents had reopened the old issue of Caroline's marriage. Although Helen lived in Cincinnati, they had been close friends from childhood, spending frequent summer and Christmas vacations together; often Helen had advised her about social complications, and they had gossiped about the girl who had a condom in her purse. Helen was wise, Caroline thought. In fact, much of the little Caroline had learned over the years came from talking and giggling with Helen late at night after parties had ended; but this was different. Caroline hardly owned the vocabulary to ask Helen her troublesome question, but as they approached the corner fruit stand, Caroline stopped walking and blurted out. "O.K., Helen, what do you know about older men . . . doing it. . . . I mean, can they? What I mean is, can women have babies if they . . . do it with older men?"

Helen had no idea what to answer. "I don't know," she stammered. They both stared at the white-aproned grocer arranging the ripe plums and peaches on the fruit stand. Suddenly Helen had an idea. "I wonder," she said, "if you could ask your doctor?"

That thought had not occurred to Caroline, and it shocked her. She could not imagine asking a strange man—even a doctor—her question. What would he think of a young single girl asking about such things? Probably he'd laugh; or if he happened to be the same age as Leon, he might be offended. She certainly couldn't do that, she thought.

Taking turns holding the crate of cherries, Helen and Caroline walked quickly back down the main street of the town chatting about the winter clothes already on display in the shop windows and avoiding the subject. But when they reached the open drawbridge near the hotel, they had to stop and wait several minutes for the sailboats to pass. Caroline could feel the chill of August: the days were getting shorter, the shadows longer, and she could see tips of red beginning to show on the sumac bushes. "My God, Helen, I guess that's what I'll have to do." She'd find a doctor . . . here in town, tomorrow. She guessed that was the only chance she had of finding out before it was too late. "Heavens, I'm almost twenty-nine years old and I'm behaving like an adolescent."

After breakfast the next morning, Caroline dressed in her most conservative gray skirt, white blouse, and walking shoes and took herself directly to the doctor's office over the pharmacy, the one they had passed the day before. She stood a moment in front of the glass door, took a deep breath, and entered the building. The hallway, dark except for the light that came in from the cloudy glass of the door, reminded her of the baggage room of a railroad station. Timidly she climbed a narrow flight of wooden stairs to the second floor, feeling ill from the mingled odors of alcohol and iodine. To her horror, there was no nurse or receptionist in the waiting room, just a dusty rubber plant, some chairs with faded slipcovers, and a table with several outdated magazines. As she turned and sat on one of the chairs, the door to the inner office suddenly opened. A gaunt, round-shouldered man with a yellow complexion and a fringe of red hair stood in the doorway beckoning her to follow him into his office. He reminded her of the illustration of Uriah Heep in her father's collection of Dickens. Oh, why hadn't she asked Helen to come. Caroline wished she could turn and run down the stairs, but before she had a chance to get up from the chair he addressed her in the kindest voice she had ever heard.

"Young lady, I am sure that you are here for a very important purpose. I can give you my professional advice. Please come into my office. Whatever it is, you must trust that I will respond honestly and confidentially. Come in, come in."

Like a schoolgirl, Caroline followed him into the office and sat in front of the huge desk crowded with papers, books, and a pipe rack with stained odd-looking pipes, one of them a long-stemmed carved meerschaum, like the one her brother George had brought home from Germany as a joke. He sat back in his chair across from her and repeated, "Trust me. Go on, tell me what brings you here."

Although the words did not pour out easily when she attempted to explain her concerns about Leon, really her parents' concerns about his age, they immediately registered with the man listening, and without waiting for her to finish, the doctor drew his chair closer to the desk, leaned toward her and spoke gently.

"My dear, you were right to come to me. Let me reassure you that a man of forty-five should be still in his prime if he is physically fit. From what you have told me, if you love this man, his ability to make you a good husband—make you physically happy—would not be a problem. And, furthermore, there is no age limit on males producing sperm."

Caroline blushed and looked down to dig into her bag for a handkerchief. When he saw her embarrassment, he got up from his chair, walked over to the window, and with his back to her asked if she had any more questions.

"No . . . no, I don't think so. You've told me what I wanted to hear. I think I'm all right now."

She dug again into her bag and pulled out her beaded change purse, but before she could open it, he turned and said, "There is no charge. Just send me a postcard from your honeymoon."

She emerged from his office feeling proud that she had defeated her own dragons and shattered the myths of her elders. Now all that was left was Leon's letter with his doctor's report, which she hoped would dispel what remained of her worry and her parents' objections. On the way back to the cottage she stopped at the specialty fruit store and shipped Leon a crate of cherries, ripe and sweet Michigan cherries, as a fitting symbol of her love for him and of her determined spirit.

Although Leon had gone immediately to his doctor, it seemed like an eternity waiting for his letter, but finally it came enclosed with the complete report for her father. Happily, the tests were negative, but most of all, Caroline was relieved about Leon's ability to respond calmly. He didn't appear to be either humiliated or angry. What he thought, she did not know, but she could hear no trace of indignation in his words. As usual, his humor prevailed as he wrote about his physical well-being, emphasizing that he was "free of social diseases" and that his "organs were healthy." To assure her of his love and faith, he also enclosed a piece of string to tie around her ring finger, "as a symbol," he said, "of their pledge to one another." His letter ended with his promising that her words "would be the truth to me against the statement of anybody else—against the adverse testimony of a multitude. . . . I have no fear, my Dearest, of your ever adjudging me wrong without giving me the benefit of a hearing." These sentences had the ring of prophecy, because the family's attacks on his character would indeed seem trivial later on when he faced more deadly accusers, legal indictment, and trial before prosecutors, judges, and jury. Yet the tendril of their faith in one another had grown into a plant with a taproot strong and deep enough to sustain their love through adversity.

As she cut through the gooseberry hedge to take a long drink of the breeze over Lake Michigan later that evening, Caroline thanked the stars that the summer would soon pass. Her family could weave no more tales to interfere with her wedding, she thought. But even as the August shadows lengthened and the summer lingered on, her father invented excuses to delay their return. First it was the New Orleans weather, then an epidemic of some crippling disease, but Leon and Caroline felt more confident that their wedding would take place before the end of September, just as they had planned. Finally, ten days after Labor Day, her father reserved compartments on the Pullman, and the family packed up their summer clothes to leave Michigan and the summer behind them.

Caroline had only two weeks to plan for her wedding, but fortunately, she had always wanted a small wedding. She never cared to be the center of attention for crowds of people she barely knew. But it was a busy two weeks, scarcely enough time for Madame Fenaceaux to finish her wedding gown or to prepare the house for the wedding—in New Orleans it was customary at the beginning of summer to remove and store curtains and rugs, to cover the furniture with slipcovers, and to place straw mats on the hardwood floors. All of these summer furnishings had to be removed before the house could be thoroughly cleaned and aired. Caroline was astounded as she watched her mother spinning through these procedures, ordering things to be done as if she and her husband had never expressed one moment of disapprobation of Leon. Caroline was so relieved, she never questioned them about their sudden change of heart; she was grateful that once they acquiesced they supported her decision, buried their old objections, and treated Leon with cordiality.

To Caroline, her parents seemed jubilant as they fitted together the parts of the wedding; probably, she thought, because it was going to take place in their new Italianate home on Audubon Place, a more fashionable neighborhood farther uptown from the old Jackson Avenue house. Audubon Place, a private circular drive with a parklike neutral ground, is enclosed at one end and guarded at the other by stone sentrylike structures and an iron arch with the words "Audubon Place" cast in ornate letters. Audubon Place served as quiet refuge for about thirty prominent New Orleanians—primarily Christian. A watchman-gatekeeper nodded to the residents as they drove in, recognizing those who belonged there, including the proper visitors. The Dreyfous family was so proud of the new house, especially Julius, who had designed it for his parents.

Even her brothers and sister participated in the wedding preparations: Julius helped direct the decorating of the room; George arranged for the beverages; and Ruth, Caroline's maid of honor, helped with folding and packing.

On September 29, Caroline, clinging to her father's arm and cradling a spray of orchids, roses, and lilies of the valley, walked down the long staircase, through the central foyer, following her bridesmaids—her sister Ruth, Julius' wife, Vera, her friend Irma Scooler, and the flower girl, her niece Carol Dreyfous, Julius and Vera's child. After entering the candlelit living room, her father let go of her arm, kissed her forehead, and sat down beside his wife in front of the massive carved-stone fireplace, a copy of one in the Doge's Palace in Venice. Caroline leaned down to kiss her mother; then, hearing the violin begin the solo they had chosen, she looked ahead, smiled, and walked down the white runner to join Leon, his brother Sol, and her brothers George and Julius. She stood next to Leon under the arbor of pink roses—no embroidered *hupa*, for this was a Reform Jewish ceremony. Shoulders touching, they joined hands, oblivious of the guests behind them. Caroline thought that Rabbi Louis Binstock's white dinner jacket and gray beard made him look a bit like God, and she felt blessed. Wearing no prayer shawl or skullcap, he spoke to them in English, murmuring only the final blessing in Hebrew. After exchanging vows quietly, they kissed discreetly and, without any other rituals, led the wedding party into the dining room.

Following the ceremony, the champagne, and the cake, Leon and Caroline left for the station. As they waited for the "All aboard," her parents kissed her and offered a few last-minute instructions about traveling; she then tore one white rose from her wilting bouquet, threw it to Ruth, and they both giggled. Soon the porter looked at his watch, gave his signal, and Leon helped her mount the steps of the Crescent Limited. There, under a shower of rice, they waved goodbye to their family and friends as the train pulled away into the night. Once out of sight of the city lights, they closed the door of their compartment and looked out at the stillness of Lake Pontchartrain as they crossed over it in the moonlight, happy that they were journeying together at last.

Later that evening, after the porter had prepared their compartment for the night, Caroline unlocked her suitcase; but when she opened it, she found to her dismay that the tray in which she had packed the new dress and white gloves that she had planned to wear upon arriving in Charleston was was not there. But what was more disheartening was that all of her trousseau, everything she needed for her wedding night, which she had so carefully folded in tissue paper—her hand-embroidered negligee with matching peignoir and white-satin mules—was in that tray back in her room at home. She wondered whether someone had made one final attempt to sabotage her happiness.

The afternoon sunshine began to fade, pauses lengthened, and as she spoke, I looked up above Mother's chair at the oval portrait of one of our ancestors. This dark painting of a large woman with stern mouth and grim eyes used to frighten me when I was alone in the room and my parents were out for the evening; but this afternoon, I saw power, not anger, a matriarch who needed to assert herself to survive as a woman in her day. I made a note to find out more about her as Mother continued talking in a voice tinted with bitterness. "I had informed my parents all along," she told me, "that despite everybody and everything I was going to marry Leon, that there was a great love in my life that had to be fulfilled . . . that their objections only made me more passionate. They could not kill what was in me."

She closed her eyes, paused for a moment, and then added: "But he was always doing favors for other people. He had such a big heart, people used him—took advantage of him. Even just before we were married Leon had signed a note for a friend's second mortgage using stock as collateral; but the friend did not meet his obligation, the stock turned out to be worthless, and the loan had to be paid. Leon had to borrow money from his brother Solly for our honeymoon." It was not to be the first or the last of Leon's errors made in good faith.

With a great sigh she continued: "My love never faltered or my courage . . . that's the way I'm built. I can give out everything but my troubles. . . .

I think of Elizabeth Barrett Browning. Do you know her poems? She waited too long . . . never had children. I always used to cheer myself up with literature through all the objections and then the troubles. . . . As I recall it, Edna St. Vincent Millay said, 'I burn my candle at both ends/It will not last the night/But oh my friends and oh my foes/It gives a wondrous light.'"

2

Ad Astra Per Aspera

𝒯he words "to the stars through effort," etched into the marble headstone, stared across at me over the wide expanse of grass that had blanketed my father for forty years. They were his translation of the Latin *ad astra per aspera,* and because they articulated his life to me, they touched me. I no longer felt any grief as I looked at the words; I only wondered about the man lying under this green carpet which, like a cloak of secrecy, covers the enigmas of his life. Its green silence hides the whole story of why, like Icarus, Daddy plunged while soaring among the stars. As Huey Long's chosen architect, Daddy designed the Louisiana state capitol and other buildings. His ideas and engineering feats became monuments and his name bespoke fame—and then ignominy.

The story of my father's rise and fall has been hushed by my family over the years, the details protected like truffles under earth and leaves. We were never told exactly what happened, but I dig away among the leaves to find what has been buried there.

Since Mother dismisses death and stays away from cemeteries, I had not visited my father's grave since his funeral, but my younger brother, Leon (my sister and I call him Bubby), and I, trying to re-create the past, ended a day last August by coming to this place. With our spouses quietly waiting behind us, we stood together in the still of the late afternoon, shadows among the stones, trying to reach the past—to bridge the gaps in our memories that have been covered with artificial silences.

On the day my father was buried here in 1953, the grass—green plastic turf—had been arranged by the undertakers around a gaping wound in the earth. As I watched them lower the coffin into that hole, I cried—that day, but not today. This day I didn't come to grieve, only to try to uncover a missing piece of the story of the man buried there. I looked at the words on the tombstone, closed my eyes, and pictured them in a higher place—the cupola of the Louisiana state capitol, where Daddy had them engraved—there near the stars.

For his resting place, Mother had chosen a replica of the art deco headstone Daddy had designed for his father's grave: it has clean lines and boxy details similar to those over and around the portal and windows of the capitol. Mother had it placed here a year after his interment, according to Jewish tradition. In selecting this headstone, my mother connected him eternally to his highest achievement, the design of the State House of Louisiana. My father had called the structure that sits atop the capitol a "temple," and in describing it, he wrote: "Thus the tower rises upward and ever upward and, at its topmost reaches, culminates in a spiritual 'Temple' symbolizing the noblest ideals of an inspired and enlightened people. . . . So it is that the crowning motif of the building is a spiritual element—a temple adorned with the representation of the things of the heavens and of the universe without: stars and moons, and symbolic winged spheres; cloud forms and nebula."

He chose the words "inspired," "enlightened," and "spiritual" to express what his structure symbolizes; to cover his mortal remains, my mother erected a monument to honor his spirit. Unlike the other ornately carved tombstones and urns in Metairie Cemetery, my father's headstone spoke to me in powerful eloquence. I stood at the foot of his grave in awkward silence.

"It's funny to see your name, Leon C. Weiss, carved on a tomb," my brother mused, breaking the silence. His remark intruded on my thoughts, telling me that we had come to this point in time and place separated by individual unspoken purposes. Even though we shared this father, we had not spoken about him since he died, and we had never talked about our shared tragedy—Daddy's incarceration. I was struck by the thought that wearing his father's name makes my brother more vulnerable to the shame and pain our family experienced; for unlike me, he identifies with the man. What must he feel about our father's guilt . . . the verdict and the sentence, I wondered. How did he deal with it then?

"How did you handle his . . . leaving us?" I asked. "You must have been only five or six at the time. Do you remember any of what you felt when he . . . was away . . . about what happened?" Of course, I used the halting phrases we had always used when referring to that time—like *incarceration.* I avoided naming the event or using the words that have to do with prison. Our family—even Betty, who never minced words—always used euphemisms: we never spoke the word *jail*—maybe *penitentiary*, but never *jail*— and it was hard to say the word *prison.* Those words conjure pictures of real criminals, felons in black and white stripes, behind bars in cement cells. Naming it made it real.

"I stayed in my room and moped. I thought it was my fault . . . that God was punishing me," he replied. "I was even told, or I thought it, that he was away at school."

Accompanied by our spouses, we had spent this sultry August day together, my brother and I, trying to reach the past, first by crossing the thirty-mile causeway over the gray expanse of Lake Pontchartrain and then to visit the grave. We had planned to find landmarks at Kiskatom, where we had spent our childhood summers. Just as we once sifted through Indian burial mounds looking for hidden treasure when we were children, my brother and I tried, like archaeologists, to unearth shards that might tell us more about ourselves and our father. I thought objects and landscapes might jar my memory. Maybe those oaks would speak to me.

I felt a bit like Rip Van Winkle as my brother drove my mother's 1976 maroon Oldsmobile down paved streets lined with groves of development houses arranged symmetrically around fake ponds and sand traps of the golf-course community Beau Chêne. While we searched for familiar trees and dirt paths of the Kiskatom that was time past, Pat and Alby followed behind. Bubby and I looked on the side of the road for the old gully, the source of the red clay that the sculptor Enrique Alferez, Daddy's friend, taught us to mold into pots and figures and bake in the sun. We trespassed across a freshly sodded lawn to find the bayou and blocked out the screams of the speedboats carving through the Tchefuncte River as we searched for pristine images we longed to see in this place that once was ours.

"Oh, look over here. Here's the well for We House," my brother called.

I walked over to a pile of broken stones and twisted pieces of pipe, and we both stared at the remains of a well from which a spout of artesian water had once bubbled. I tried to smell the sulphur and hear the sound of running

water, remembering hot summers and thirst-quenching waters of my childhood, but the source of this spring was buried underground. We looked
around for We House but found only broken fragments of cement and the
creosoted remains of pilings that had held the dock we fished from. We
House (not "Wee House") was so named by my father because I mixed up
pronouns, using *we* instead of *our*. We House consisted of a boathouse with
a screened-in large room upstairs where we slept on cots, read by kerosene
lamps, listened to Daddy's animal tales, cooked on a wood-burning stove,
and rolled down canvas awnings when summer storms threatened our
nights. We camped in this house while Big House was being built, spending
weekends exploring the river or plowing our pirogue through the water
hyacinths on the bayou, fishing for trout or perch among the cypress knees
and the tall duck grass that grew in the shallows at the edge of the bayou.
The leafy path from the river led us through live oaks—our picnic oaks—
past an unpainted shack where another family lived before the land was
ours. Daddy had told us they were squatters, Hungarians. Although the
word *squatter* was as foreign to me as these people, I remember gaunt faces
with grim eyes that stared at us and bony legs that stuck out from tattered
clothes. One day, they and their dwelling disappeared. I never asked, but I
wondered about them and where they went. Years later, when I read *Grapes
of Wrath*, the image of their faces reappeared like a sepia photograph, faded
and torn.

Once Big House was built on a rise away from the river, only the mo-
torboat, pirogues, and bamboo fishing rods lived in We House; we went to
the river less often, spending long summer days around the swimming pool,
learning to perfect our swan dives and jackknives or washing our hair under
the spout at the shallow end of the pool. One summer Daddy encouraged
me to try a back dive: he held my waist as I stood at the edge of the diving
board, leaning backward lower and lower. Suspended upside down, my
hands reaching for the water, I saw, inverted, the numerals "1937" carved
into the granite marker over the spout at the shallow end. I wasn't afraid,
because his strong hands supported my back until I almost touched the
water; each time, my body dropped in a perfect arc into the water until I
was ready to lean back and dive on my own. But the pool and the well that
fed it have been filled in and now are covered by some other children's
grassy playground.

As my brother and I stood by the bank of the river that August day, I looked toward the bend that jutted out on the left and wondered how long it used to take us to round that bend and reach Madisonville in our clumsy rowboat with outboard motor. When we went there, we used to shop for chicken feed and canned vegetables at the country store. While Daddy selected the supplies, I spent my tooth fairy money on comic books and bubble gum. We went on these boating excursions often with Daddy but never while he was away. No one else could pull the rope that jumped the motor or take it apart and make it work when it rusted. . . .

I looked at my watch and remembered we had promised Mother we'd be home for dinner. "We gotta go, Bubby," I said, but it was hard to pull him away from where he stood, bemused. He was lost in his own faraway memories—perhaps thinking of when he and his friend Bernard hunted alligators in the marshy shallows along the brown river. Small ones, I guess, since Bubby said he wrestled them, grabbed them by the neck, while Bernard tied their legs—or was this another tall tale? I tried again. "Maybe we can find oyster loaves in Madisonville. I'd like to see what's become of that sleepy town, anyhow. We could eat them by the river. Come on, you all."

I looked at him and tried to remember him as the little brother who loved trailing after his father, trying so hard to emulate him. He still had a faraway and melancholy look. I wanted to cheer him. "You know what Robert Kornfeld, Cecilia Seiferth's husband, told me at a party the last time I was down here? He recalled enjoying a scrumptious duck dinner on his first visit to Kiskatom. He told me that just as he was finishing his last bite he turned to Mother to rave about the marvelous duck dinner, but before she could respond, you piped up and commented, 'Yeah, and they had to kill Quackie to do it.' I guess you made a hit, for he never forgot that moment. . . . My God, that must have been over fifty years ago."

"I was just thinking," he said, without looking my way, "how Daddy tried growing plants to sell . . . to make Kiskatom a nursery and cover some of the expenses . . . after he came back. We built a greenhouse, grew boxwood and ligustrum. We baled the plants, and a van came from Texas to truck them away. After Daddy . . . died, I kept it going for a while. I came here every weekend my first year of college . . . worked with the caretakers . . . but then it was sold."

Leaving the remains of our remembered landscape to the golfers and speedboaters, we drove past the old barn, now converted into someone else's house, past the pigeon house, also transformed into the tower wing of a stranger's home, away from the river, beyond the gates of our childhood, with hardly a backward glance.

Now standing here in the cemetery after our journey to Kiskatom, I felt weary from the sun, beer, oyster loaves, and distances we'd crossed in time and space. It saddened me to think that perhaps all too soon I'd be back in this graveyard, standing in front of this grassy plot . . . but I brushed those thoughts away and took one long look at the name in the fading light, knowing that now we needed to leave. As we turned away from the grave and my brother walked ahead toward the car, my sister-in-law grabbed my arm and whispered, "Leta, I don't believe it. In all the forty years I've known your brother, he's never . . . ever . . . even mentioned a word about your father. Leon has never spoken to me about his father."

After breakfast next morning, I brought my cup of coffee upstairs to Mother's room and sat on the end of her bed, near her chair. With her arms and back bolstered with pillows, she sat with head turned toward the open window. Her cloudy blue eyes seemed to look at the sun and at the breeze playing with the filmy curtains and ruffling the pile of magazines on the table next to her reclining chair. I sat and watched her struggling to hold her cup with arthritic fingers that refused to bend.

"Mother, what was it like when Daddy was so involved with the building of the capitol . . . with Huey Long?"

She didn't answer for some time and then said tersely, "Oh, I don't remember. I blotted all that out. I led a double life. I only wanted to take care of my children and house. I didn't take any active part in politics."

"But Mother, you were there . . . when the buildings were finally opened . . . at celebrations."

After a few moments of silence, she turned her head away from the shifting curtains and grinned, "Yes, we did go to the dedication of the capitol. . . . It was just after you were born. We took you in a basket. And the nurse. It was funny. Our friends, Elise and Jake Levy, couldn't get a hotel room so they ended up sleeping on the floor in our room. It was some *ménage*! In the middle of the night I had to get up to nurse you—you were in the next room with the nurse, and I forgot about Elise and Jake, and I practically fell on top of them. We laughed so. Then at the dedication in front of the capitol, your sister had to go to the bathroom just as Leon was introduced and was about to give his speech. Mother—your grand-mother—carried her back to the hotel and they missed the entire ceremony . . . and I had to rush right back to our rooms and nurse you. . . . I left just as the applause ended."

Applause rang in Caroline's ears that day, May 16, 1932, as Leon, standing on the granite steps of the capitol, addressed the crowds on the capitol grounds below. His words, which rang out from the massive bronze doors, proclaimed "that the building" had been erected to "express in stone, granite, bronze, and marble and in other enduring materials, the colorful history of this once unbounded dominion, the struggling colony, and now the pro-gressive and powerful State." The applause resounded in her ears as she walked away from the impressive event, through the crowds back to the hotel. As she sat by the window of her hotel room, holding her new baby, her second daughter—me—she thought about the day when this phase of their life began.

1928

Caroline and Leon had been married less than a year when the Barnett Building, the proud store the firm had worked on all year, was dedicated. The streets of the city steamed from the intense July heat and the early morning shower as they walked from the car to the glass front of the build-ing and entered through a door under a decorative arch two stories high. They were among the first to arrive, since Caroline hated being late. Leon took her by the hand and guided her proudly around the freshly painted rooms.

"It's perfect," she exclaimed.

"I wish they'd gotten rid of the trash outside. I told them to finish hauling away those scraps of carpet," Leon replied nervously. He reached under his coat jacket, took a Camel and a paper match folder from his shirt pocket, scratched the match with one hand army-style, and took a long drag. "I knew we were going to be too early." After a few more deep drags, he crushed his cigarette out in one of the chrome ash stands placed around the room, led her to a folding chair near one of the large fans, and took the handwritten page from his pocket to look over his speech once again. He always wrote out his speeches, choosing eloquent words to reflect his profound beliefs, his spirituality. His language sounded ornate sometimes, even archaic, in contrast to the contemporary designs of his buildings; but he loved words, even reading the thesaurus in his spare time. During his undergraduate days at Tulane, he had written poems and stories, some of which were published in the university's literary magazine. He took great care in preparing and presenting his lectures for the courses he taught as professor of engineering at Tulane. Once, when lecturing about the design of libraries, he began with a carefully researched history of libraries of the world before addressing the technical aspect of design.

"Oh, there's Julius and Solis," Caroline declared. "Come sit here," she called to her brother, Julius, and to the third partner in the firm, Solis Seiferth. They came over and sat down. Julius, perspiring profusely, loosened his collar and patted his forehead with a large handkerchief embroidered with his initials. While they chatted, the room began to fill with businessmen in blue suits and wives dressed too warmly for this July morning. As people settled close to the fans, waiting for the ceremony to begin, a large man in a straw hat, rumpled pin-striped suit, and green silk tie pushed his way through the row of chairs and settled himself uncomfortably on the too-small seat next to Solis.

Leon had never met Huey Long, but as state commander of the Military Order of the World War, that past April, before the election, he had written to Long recommending the appointment of a colleague for adjutant general of the state. Leon didn't think that Long would remember him or the letter.

Huey Long turned to Solis, shook his hand, and congratulated him on the beauty of this new building. Solis thanked him and added, "Mr. Long, I'd like you to meet the head of our firm, Leon Weiss."

"Leon Weiss! Why in heaven haven't you been after me to do some work for me? Every blasted architect in the state of Louisiana has been bothering me. I'd like you to design my house. You get in touch with me, hear?"

"Mr. Long," Leon responded flatly, looking around Julius at the governor's smiling face. "I have to tell you . . . I didn't even vote for you."

"Mr. Weiss, that's all right, you design me a house. You stay out of my politics, and I'll stay out of your architecture. I've got great plans for this state. You're the best damn architect in the state, and I'm gonna need your help."

As Mr. Barnett was tapping the water glass on the lectern and a hush was settling over the room, Leon had no chance to answer except to end the exchange with a whispered promise to send him some sketches. While waiting for the first speech, Leon suddenly remembered what Huey Long had said in his campaign speech in St. Martinville, in Acadian country, a few months ago: "And it is here under this oak where Evangeline waited for her lover, Gabriel. This oak is immortal, but Evangeline is not the only one who waited here in disappointment. Where are the schools, the roads and highways, the institutions for the disabled you sent your money to build?" His words reverberated in Leon's head all that day as the heat and the celebration continued, and they echoed once again late in the evening as he and Caroline sat quietly alone in their apartment after dinner at Antoine's, with the Seiferths, the Barnetts, and Julius and Vera.

Now that the draftsmen had completed the plans for their new home on Dominican Street and Caroline had selected most of the decor, Leon could turn his attention to creating preliminary sketches for the governor's mansion. His draftsmen sharpened their pencils and began.

1929

After Leon's exhausting winter of work and anxiety-filled spring helping Caroline through the difficult months of pregnancy, their first child, Betty, was born prematurely, in July, 1928. These were anxious days as they waited at home for their new one to be discharged from the hospital. It also meant that Caroline had to pump breast milk instead of nursing her baby. She was not only exhausted from giving birth but despondent as well. Although she was relieved when the baby finally weighed enough to come home, she faced what loomed as enormous pressure—the thought of moving into their new Dominican Street house. She tried to focus on her joys—the thrill when the doctor confirmed that she was expecting—the relief she and Leon felt after the doubts and fears about being able to conceive that had blocked their union not so long ago. Gradually, as the first year passed, her body felt strong again and her former spirit returned. She was pleased and proud when Leon and Huey Long signed the agreement to build the governor's mansion on November 7, 1929.

That morning, after signing the papers in Leon's busy office in the Maison Blanche Building on Canal Street, Long grabbed Leon's arm and said, "Come on over to the Roosevelt. I'll treat you to some potlikker and corn bread. I'll meet you in the coffee shop. We'll talk about this building and some other plans I have."

Not being too fond of watery, greasy greens, Leon ordered a bowl of gumbo, French bread, and a crisp green salad; and he listened as Long talked about his plans for the university, for a new capitol, and for a hospital—all of which he intended for Leon's firm, Weiss, Dreyfous and Seiferth, to design.

But Leon had worried all that spring about the flood of controversy enveloping Huey Long. He and Caroline listened to the radio as the tide against Long intensified. They spent their evenings listening to the news and reading newspaper accounts of the impeachment proceedings. Dinner-table conversations with friends now were heated debates for and against the governor. Sometimes the subject had to be dropped after it became too intense—often the wives intervened by interjecting a topic that might divert the flow of conversation. Because of the magnitude of their rancor, the anti-Long group in New Orleans ostracized those who supported Long or were involved with his administration, splitting the community and breaking up friendships. Caroline and Leon's good friends, Thomas Jefferson Feibleman (Jeff) and his wife, Lillian, argued vociferously, with Jeff calling Long a dictator and Leon trying to convince him of Long's vision for the state, that focus of Long's complicated politics which Leon believed in; but Jeff's beliefs were too extreme—too aristocratic, Caroline thought. After Leon's involvement with Long ended, they renewed their friendship with the Feiblemans, and the women remained close friends until Lillian's death, years later.

Lillian and Jeff's daughter Bonnie and I were good friends—best friends during these years, even though she went to a different private school—Country Day—a progressive one, and I went to Isidore Newman School. I always wondered why our parents weren't friends, because Bonnie and I spent so many weekends together either at Kiskatom or at her parents' country home, which they named La Brush because it was located in Lacombe, a little town near Slidell.

The political scene changed my parents' social life somewhat, although some other good friends—like Leon Cahn, who hated Long—didn't allow politics to cause a breach in their relationship. Most everyone they knew who was not involved with Long opposed him; a few believed in his ideology, whereas others supported him for practical reasons—knowing that siding with the Long administration meant financial gain. Many business and professional people in the city wanted to be dealt in, for these were hard times for making a living. Estelle, the wife of Leon's brother Sol, urged her husband to join with Long because she thought they could make lots of money, but Sol wasn't tempted; he did not like Long's tactics. On the topic of Huey Long, no neutral ground existed. Some people were envious of those who worked for the Long administration. Others, feeling that an association with Long would taint them, wanted no connection with him. Felix did not like Long's politics and kept his distance.

Alfred Danziger, Felix's nephew, became Long's social and political friend, however. On several occasions Alfred invited Huey to parties at his studio in the Pontalba building where he often entertained French Quarter guests. Apparently, one night a scantily dressed showgirl sat on Huey's lap and inquired, "What's ya name, Honey?"

Long answered, "I'm Huey Long."

She replied, "Sure, and I'm Franklin Roosevelt." Wanting to prove his identity to her, Long picked up the phone and called the National Guard. Different versions of the story appeared in the newspapers during the impeachment proceedings.

Leon's relationship with Long remained professional. Although Leon believed in Long's vision and perhaps was even seduced by his powerful charisma, he and Caroline were not socially involved with Long or with any of his close associates—people like Abe Shushan or Seymour Weiss. At home at the dinner table, Caroline and Leon hosted literary and artistic friends, some of whom were visitors to the city. At one of these occasions E. C. Lindeman, a contributing editor to the *New Republic,* vehemently castigated Long; but before the evening ended, Leon believed that his defense of Long had softened Lindeman's opinion. Leon had told him flatly that "he was not acquainted with the facts or he would not have formed his conclusions so readily; that the newspaper accounts of this case were not reliable." Later, in a letter to Long, Leon repeated what he had said to Lindeman and enclosed copies of Lindeman's editorial entitled "Impeachment or Persecution in Louisiana." Leon ended his letter by telling Long that "I have been very busy in an unobtrusive way in spreading your gospel where I am certain it is resulting in favorable sentiment toward you." In 1929, Huey P. Long was impeached but not convicted.

That winter, as the baby was almost weaned, Caroline felt the renewal of her energy when sleep became less frequently interrupted. With fewer demands on her time and a competent nurse to help with Betty, the anxiety she and Leon both felt for their baby's health began to dissipate. Caroline appreciated her mother's coming every day, carrying lunch upstairs so Caroline could relax on the chaise longue. Julia helped with the mending or played with her new grandchild while Caroline rested. Caroline began again to feel a surge of energy and spirit; with it came an eagerness to work with Leon. She longed for the excitement of helping him design the interior of the new mansion.

Ever since their wedding day, which had taken place on a Thursday, Leon had remembered their special day by bringing her a present every Thursday. He called it the "Thursday gift." One raw January day, after a long afternoon of meetings and negotiations, on the way to the parking garage on Iberville Street, Leon stopped and picked up a package at Loubat's, a wholesale restaurant supply store in the French Quarter, on Bienville Street near the river. He next dropped by the Acme Oyster House to order freshly opened oysters at the marble-topped bar and went to retrieve his car. As he drove down St. Charles Avenue, impatient to get home, he glanced occasionally at the oysters, the package from Loubat's, and a roll of blueprints for the mansion.

Not expecting Leon so early, Caroline was upstairs rocking the baby. He stood still in the hall at the foot of the stairs, listening to the creak of the rocker and her voice singing *Fais-do-do* . . . remembering . . . remembering for a moment his other first-born . . . but that was over. Caroline had washed that away. Hesitating no longer, he handed the oysters to Tonbeck, the new cook, and rushed up the stairs to kiss Caroline and give her the Thursday gift.

Caroline put the baby in her crib and ripped open the package. "Oh, they're beautiful," she exclaimed as she tore away the tissue from each of the red crystal water and wine goblets. "We'll use them Saturday. The crowd is coming and they'll be twelve for dinner . . . perfect! I've never seen anything like these." After holding one in front of the lighted lamp, she stood up and they kissed. Carefully she returned the glasses to the box and said, "Go on down. Dinner's ready. I just need to fix my hair."

That night, after Tonbeck had cleared the dinner dishes from the table, Leon spread out the blueprints. As they perused them and talked, they began to see the rooms of the governor's mansion come alive. From the tiles with handpainted water lilies for the bathrooms, just like the ones Leon had ordered from Italy for their own house, to the French handpainted American landscapes for the walls of the dining room, ideas began to flower into lists and sketches. While Leon drew, Caroline wrote down items to purchase and places to shop for wallpaper and furniture. They studied the plans until far past midnight. Leon fixed himself a bourbon and soda, smoked his last cigarette of the evening, and turned off the lamps in the living room. Before going upstairs to bed, they stood for a moment in the solarium looking out at the mossy limbs of the oak tree and at the newly planted camellias in the moonlit garden.

3
The 1930s

With the construction of the governor's mansion underway, Caroline haunted the antique stores on Royal Street, finding, among other items, two large mirrors for the living room. Designing the children's rooms kindled her enthusiasm as she rummaged through the antique shops' cluttered back rooms, discovering treasures. Her best finds were for the Longs' little girl Rose's room: a canopy bed, a dressing table, a burled wood desk, and a sewing table and chair. For the sons' rooms, she had found handsome dressers and beds. Once she had finished selecting the wall coverings and curtains for these rooms, working with Marc and Lucille Anthony, she began to plan with them the formal public rooms. They chose fine damask and velvet for the drapery and huge crystal chandeliers to hang in the Louis XVI East Room and the state dining room. Even when she was home and sitting on the terrace watching Betty's amusing antics, her thoughts were of the mansion's soon-to-be-planted sunken gardens and the still-to-be-furnished rooms.

Once, before the mansion was finished, Leon again bounded up the stairs with news for Caroline. "We're building the capitol! I've just met with Long. We've decided to build a skyscraper. I'm going up to Nebraska to see that nearly completed skyscraper capitol and talk to the contractors who worked with Bertram Goodhue, the architect. And I met with Dr. James Monroe Smith, the president of LSU. We're doing some designs for new dorms. The legislature adopted a million-dollar construction program." His breathless voice startled her, for she was accustomed to his normally calm demeanor and careful speech. Although Caroline foresaw late hours and long working weeks, she too was thrilled. She put aside the book she was reading and went downstairs with him for dinner.

Leon took the train for Nebraska the following Monday. Knowing that he'd have a whole day in Chicago between connecting trains, he had contacted Frank Lloyd Wright and arranged to meet the man for whom he held such admiration. Speaking to Caroline on the phone that night, Leon reported the day's adventure. He told her that he had taken a taxi to Wright's house, rung the doorbell, and waited. After what seemed an eternity, an attractive woman opened the door.

"I'm here to see Mr. Wright," Leon announced.

"He's not here," the woman, apparently his wife, replied.

"Can you tell me where he is?"

"Lord, I wish I knew. If you could tell me, I'd indeed be grateful!"

Leon told Caroline that he had chuckled all the way back to the hotel. "I knew Wright had a scandalous reputation, but I didn't think he'd miss an appointment in the middle of the afternoon." Leon never did have another opportunity to meet Frank Lloyd Wright, but he enjoyed retelling the story of why Wright stood him up. That experience became part of his repertoire of favorite anecdotes.

After arriving the next evening in Lincoln, Nebraska, he checked into his hotel and took a cab to the nearly completed state capitol. While the taxi waited, he stood in the cold in the moonlight and gazed in wonderment at the impressive skyscraper as ideas and plans flickered about in his imagination. That night, he hardly slept as he rehearsed questions for the contractors responsible for this building. He wanted their technical advice, for he now had his moonlight inspiration. As the train rattled south late the following afternoon, he envisioned what would shortly become the capitol of the state of Louisiana.

As soon as he arrived home, Leon gave his notebook full of sketches to his artist, Byron Proctor, who transformed them into a final rendering for presentation to the governor and to the board of liquidation on March 1. On receiving their approval, Leon's office began drawing up the plans and designing a plastic model of the building. He and his partners took the train or drove the swampy road to Baton Rouge many times over the next few months, looking at the site, meeting with officials, and supervising the engineers and draftsmen.

The regular staff in the office had put away the drawings for the mansion, which was almost finished, and began the huge project now facing them.

New draftsmen had to be hired as well as additional skilled engineers, but the specifications and artistic details belonged to the architects. Leon, Solis, and Julius spent hours with legislators and government experts, detailing the designs for the senate, house of representatives, and courtrooms. The details had to be summarized in carefully composed volumes of specifications. By November 8, all of the documents and plans would be completed and the whole project on the market for the call for bids a month later. Eight months after it was endorsed by Long, the project was approved by the voters. The office then completed the ninety pages of drawings and four hundred pages of specifications—a total of eighty thousand mimeographed sheets and twenty thousand blueprints.

Hoping the bids would come in low enough to include his dream for sculpture to adorn the building, Leon came home late each evening laden with volumes of Louisiana history he had selected from his favorite French Quarter bookseller. He and his partners researched patterns for grillwork, marble and stone for façades, and planned the placement of sculpture. This was not the end of the task, however; sculptors, artists, and craftsmen would need to be selected, a process that would take months.

The winter day in 1930 when the sealed bids for the capitol were opened, stillness lay like a mist over the room, and Leon prayed silently that the bids would come in low enough so that the sculpture he envisioned could be included. He felt disappointed, however, that Caroline could not come up to Baton Rouge to share the excitement of opening the sealed bids with Huey Long, but she had to stay home with a feverish child and wait for Doctor Blum. Leon would memorize all the details of the afternoon and share them later.

Oh, well, Caroline thought, as she took her new blue silk dress from the closet. It's Leon's birthday, and our good friends Elise and Jake and some of the others are coming for dinner. We'll hear Leon describe the event with his usual ability to remember all the specifics. She thought tonight they'd celebrate both occasions with a special dinner. Having set the table, given last-minute instructions to Tonbeck about serving the shrimp creole, she bathed and went back downstairs in her dressing gown to wait at the open front door for the newspaper to arrive. The sun was shining, even though it was a cold December 10.

At last she heard the delivery boy whistling as he came around the azalea bushes and up the path with the paper in hand. She took it from him, opened it, and saw Leon's face staring back at her. On the front page of the afternoon paper, Leon's photograph and Huey Long's appeared on either side of a drawing of the capitol. She brought the newspaper upstairs and read that the low bidder was the George A. Fuller Company of Washington, D.C., and that work would begin the following Monday. She couldn't wait for Leon to come home and tell her all about the afternoon. She worried, however, about the busy year that loomed ahead; she knew about late hours and frantic deadlines, but what she did not know was that Leon would be climbing around checking construction on scaffolding ten stories high. Wanting to think of the capitol as Leon did, she would try not to see it as an intrusion in her life. So much work lay ahead of him, with so many decisions to make . . . and all the other LSU buildings. But she knew he'd include her in planning the details.

Leon did take Caroline with him on several trips, one of them to an Indiana quarry, the only source of limestone with the special tone and grain that Leon had seen a sample of. He wanted to choose for himself the limestone that would be used as structural material for the capitol. They spent several days on a tour of the quarry, following John Edgeworth, vice president of the company, and looking at different stones. One misty morning, while standing and looking out over miles of limestone quarries, Caroline exclaimed, "Oh, the whole scene is so impressive. It reminds me of the ruins of ancient Greece."

John Edgeworth turned to her and smiled. "In all these years of looking at this glorious sight, I've never heard anyone make that connection, but you're absolutely right."

The friendship between the two men had begun that fall, when they met for the first time. During one busy Friday in November, the office was crowded with men who had traveled far to compete for work on this building, for these were Depression times, and winning a contract for work meant survival. Leon had been busy all day talking to stone and marble vendors when the telephone rang. He picked up the receiver, turned away from the desk, and heard a man's anxious voice asking to speak to Mr. Weiss. Cupping one hand over his other ear, Leon heard the voice on the other end saying something about a broken foot.

"Who is this?" Leon asked.

"John Edgeworth . . . Indiana limestone. I've sprained my foot. I'm laid up at the hotel. I can't get my shoe on. I can't come to your office. I—"

"You stay right there. I'll come right up there to you."

Deserting the other men who were crowding around his desk eager to speak to him and land a contract, Leon went over to the hotel to talk to Edgeworth and see samples of the limestone from Indiana. After they had discussed limestone, costs, and other factors, Leon knew he wanted to deal with this man, not only for his superior limestone but because he also liked and trusted him. Before returning to his office, Leon awarded him the contract. Edgeworth never got over the fact that a busy architect would leave his office full of people to see "a poor wounded contractor in his hotel bedroom." The meeting resulted in an order of eight carloads of limestone from Victor Oolitic Stone Company for the sculptured groups for the front of the capitol; Leon's visit to the hotel to see John Edgeworth had carved the first layer of a long-lasting friendship, one based on mutual respect and trust. This man would return the favor a few years later by coming back south to testify at his friend's trial.

Days were spent evaluating proposals, selecting the skillful, and weeding out those who would not be given contracts. Leon and his partners spent three or four mornings a week listening to the men who had come to compete for the work. One day, he met with some people from Cincinnati eager to do the glasswork. They had come into the office early. One of them, a ruddy-complected man with red hair, placed his large hand with two fingers missing on the plans spread out on Leon's desk. He leaned toward Leon and whispered, "We're used to paying kickbacks, ya know." He grinned at Leon through cracked lips and waited.

Leon got up from his chair and stared across the desk at the man. Though he felt his face flush with rage, Leon checked his anger and said in a quiet voice, "And you are the kind we don't want to work with." With that, he turned from his desk and pointed to the door. He had tried hard to find the best glass people, and these men were highly thought of.

One sunny December morning, Caroline was out in the garden picking camellias for the dining room table when she was called to the telephone.

It was Leon. "How would you like to go to New York? Do you think you could manage to get things ready so we can leave the day after tomorrow? I need to look at Piccirilli's bronzes."

Caroline thought a moment, visualizing her schedule for the week. Then she replied, "Oh, I'd love to. I'm sure Ruth would stay here, and there's nothing I really have to do. Yes, I'll go with you."

Leon and Caroline traveled to New York to meet Atillio Piccirilli at his studio in the Bronx, where he and his four brothers worked. They arrived in the morning at Pennsylvania Station. Not having been in New York for at least four years, Caroline had forgotten the crowds and the thrill of Manhattan. Although Leon wanted to hurry to the hotel and expressed his impatience, Caroline persuaded him to ask the taxi driver to take a quick detour so she could just glance at her favorite shops along Fifth Avenue. As they drove past, Caroline gazed through the frosty cab windows at the sparkling display of fashions, mentally listing the shops she'd invade the next morning. She hoped she'd have time to buy some gowns for the Christmas season. There were several invitations waiting on her desk at home. She'd go to her favorite linen shop on Madison Avenue to look at sheets and tablecloths; but first she'd have to purchase some rubber galoshes to protect her feet from this unfamiliar snow and ice.

Once they had settled into their hotel room and ordered theater tickets for their free evenings, Caroline bathed and dressed, and they hailed a cab for Mr. Piccirilli's studio. Arriving at the brownstone building, they pushed open the door and climbed the long flight of stairs to the garret. When the sculptor opened his door, Caroline gasped at the forest of sculptures and grillwork, some still unfinished. The room smelled of varnish, metal, and dust, but she loved the smell of art in process.

They were greeted with a wide smile and a warm handshake by a stocky man about Leon's height, with a full head of dark hair and a trimmed mustache. He took Leon by the arm, offered them a vermouth, and guided them through the maze of stone and metal. Caroline had never seen works of art in such quantity except in museums. While the men talked, she circled the room once again.

Late that evening, after eating huge plates of pasta at a neighborhood restaurant, Leon and Caroline looked over Piccirilli's proposals, and by the end of the meal, Leon had invited him to bring his sketches to the office as soon as he could make the trip to New Orleans.

As the work progressed on the capitol building, Dominican Street became a lively salon for artists and writers. Caroline was enchanted with the assortment of new friends she now included with some of her old ones at their dinner parties. Their social life consisted of gatherings of literary and artistic people and engaging conversations.

Some of her former acquaintances, part of the Uptown crowd, belonged to the Jewish country club, but even though Caroline played tennis and golf, neither she nor Leon was interested in joining private clubs. They just didn't enjoy the country club scene and did not aspire to membership in elite groups—either Jewish or Christian. Since Leon disliked large gatherings and thought that noisy cocktail parties and formal balls were tedious affairs, they were not looking for invitations to fashionable events.

Some prominent Jewish families in the city wanted to be included in Gentile social life and rather expected to be invited to join prestigious organizations, such as the Boston Club and the Southern Yacht Club, since people in the generation before theirs had been active members. In the thirties, however, these clubs closed their doors to even the most respected Jewish men. Because her brother George liked sailing, it angered him when he was denied membership in the same yacht club that had welcomed his father two decades before. Caroline and Leon never felt excluded from anything—even during Mardi Gras, when a few of the extremely wealthy Jewish families left town to avoid embarrassment at not being invited to attend Mardi Gras balls or ride on floats—particularly those of Momus and Comus, elite clubs that once also sponsored parades. Caroline and Leon didn't try to conceal the fact that they were Jewish, as did some families with social ambitions. They belonged to Temple Sinai, and although being affiliated with a Jewish temple was meaningful to them, they felt no need to attend services regularly. Like many of their contemporaries and some of their parents' generation, they shunned organized religion. They didn't join committees or observe religious festivals—except Passover, when Felix and Julia invited them for a family *seder.*

Caroline and Leon were content with being part of an intellectual crowd of mavericks who were drawn together by their interests in art and literature and not by artificial classifications: money, religion, nationality, or the number of generations one's ancestors had lived in the city. Although they never pretended they were anyone else, they had their own brand of snobbery: they were intellectuals, felt secure with people like themselves, and had no desire to move into any other world—perhaps their exclusiveness generated feelings of jealousy in outsiders who weren't invited in, but they weren't aware of that. When Mardi Gras came, they celebrated with their friends— roaming the French Quarter after the parades, mingling with the maskers and suppressing their laughter at female impersonators until later in the evening, while at home drinking highballs. Good food, strong whiskey, and the flow of ideas and laughter satisfied them completely.

When building the house, Leon had included a large locked closet in the pantry of their kitchen; he fashioned it to hold the bootleg liquor that somehow found its way to their house. In New Orleans in those days, whiskey came by boat, was picked up at the docks by someone, then tested by a chemist for safety, and surreptitiously transported to private homes. Customers needed a large storage space, because it was safer to have infrequent deliveries. Drinking and storytelling sessions lasted late into the night at Caroline and Leon's.

On one of these occasions, an unusually warm March afternoon in 1931, the table was set with a white damask cloth, the red crystal glasses, and her freshly polished silver. Caroline picked the last few Purple Dawn camellias and arranged them in a silver bowl, which she placed on a blue mirror on the table. Tonbeck was busy in the kitchen stuffing the heads of crawfish for the bisque that they would serve for dinner, for Leon had invited the sculptors who had been in the city all week. That evening Lorado Taft, Adolph Weinman, the Ulric Ellerhusens, and Angela Gregory were coming, in addition to their usual crowd of friends: the Roark Bradfords, the Thad St. Martins, the Lyle Saxons, and the Marc Anthonys. Caroline felt that the new guests would enjoy a special creole dish, and she was eager to hear the artists talk about their work. She hoped they might even bring some of their sketches, since they had been in New Orleans most of the week negotiating with the partners for the capitol's sculpture. She had already seen Taft's models for his enormous statues, *The Pioneers* and *The Patriots*, which would stand on buttresses on the entrance steps. Leon had also given the task of sculpturing some relief heads for the capitol to Angela

Gregory as a tribute to her father, a close friend and professor for whom he had been a teaching assistant. Leon remembered her as a child, admired her work, and wanted to help her career.

As Caroline placed the napkins, arranged the placecards in porcelain flowered holders, and admired the red crystal glasses that sparkled in the light from the brass chandelier, she smiled as she thought about Ulric Ellerhusen using Betty's face as a model for one of the casket girls on the historical frieze planned for the exterior of the building. Caroline envisioned her little girl carved in stone, taking her place as one of the young orphan girls sent from France to marry Louisiana pioneers. In the frieze, these young women, holding caskets packed with all their possessions, stand before a group of Ursuline nuns and wait to be given in holy matrimony to some unknown pioneer man. Although Caroline hated thinking about these poor lonely girls, she liked thinking of Betty's being included in one of the stories of Louisiana's history. On the façade of the capitol, Betty would be honored along with Judah Benjamin, Jefferson, Tulane, Audubon, and other prominent figures.

Caroline was looking forward to the evening. She liked listening to the artists, and she expected that Roark Bradford might again tell stories—some from his new book, *Ol' Man Adam an' His Chillun*—and perhaps Thad would tell a few jokes in Cajun dialect. He always captivated people with his wonderful storytelling. Certainly the evening would be filled with art and literature and plenty of laughter.

There would be many such occasions as the building progressed. Caroline and Leon held special dinners at their home, sitting at the table long after dessert, sometimes sipping café brûlot, a strong black brew flavored with illegal liquor and flamed in a big silver bowl at the table. Other evenings, Caroline and Leon had supper at Roark Bradford's French Quarter house on Toulouse Street. There they mingled with his writer friends: Grace King, Lillian Hellman, Lyle Saxon, and the founders of the literary journal the *Double Dealer*—Julius Friend, John McClure, and Basil Thompson. Sometimes other writers who lived in or visited the city dropped in—Sherwood Anderson, William Faulkner, or F. Scott Fitzgerald. Caroline and Leon often left at dawn, laughing all the way home after an evening of Brad's stories—most of which would be considered racist today. Other nights were spent at the Arts and Crafts Club on Royal Street, attending

lectures or viewing exhibitions. Sometimes they dined at Galatoire's or Ar-
naud's after lectures or before seeing plays at Le Petit Théâtre.

Some evenings they dressed formally for dinner parties. Caroline relished
wearing long gowns, especially the new white one with silver spangles for
which she had received so many compliments. She had a difficult time
getting Leon to wear his tuxedo, however, so on the night of a formal party,
she'd greet him with a big highball and then "he acted like a little lamb."
Sometimes, he even sang "Button Up Your Overcoat" or "Makin' Whoopee"
all the way downtown; or he'd tell her again for the fiftieth time the story
about the time his clutch failed and he had to drive down St. Charles
Avenue in reverse, all the way home.

One Sunday afternoon, Caroline and Leon drove across the lake to Thad
St. Martin's house. He cooked a fabulous courtbouillon that evening to
celebrate having finished the final chapter of his book *Madame Toussaint's
Wedding Day*. Glad, as his wife was nicknamed, and guests watched as Thad
chopped parsley, shallots, garlic, and onions for the roux while telling his
story of the people who lived on Bayou Chien-Loup. Caroline wished the
day would never end as they listened to the woes of Madame Toussaint and
défint (deceased) Toussaint, her former husband, Cajun characters from the
new book. They roared with laughter at Thad, gesturing with parsley-
coated hands slippery with lard, as he described Madame Toussaint and
Jean jumping over the new broom as part of their wedding ceremony and
spending their wedding night in their oyster boat repairing the motor by
candlelight.

4
The Noblest Work

*F*ourteen months from December 17, 1930, the day Huey Long had turned the first spadeful of earth, the capitol was completed, and the beacon in the temple structure at the top of the tower was lit. Eight days later, on February 25, 1932, I was born. Mine was an easier birth for my mother than my sister's had been as there were no complications this time. In fact, my Aunt Ruth told me she was afraid Mother wouldn't make it to the hospital, I was coming so fast, but Ruth got her there just in time. Daddy bounded in as soon as he received the news, bringing Mother a gift of yellow roses and a diamond watch he had ordered from Adler's. He marveled at the sight of Caroline holding her new little girl. He felt particularly moved since he hadn't thought Caroline could carry another baby to term. So resigned were they to that certainty, they had designed their new home on Dominican Street for only one child. Two little sisters, though, could share one room.

Two births for my mother and father to celebrate that spring—mine and the capitol's. Once Mother and I were safely home and the capitol completed, they could look forward to the celebration of its opening in two months. Mother realized that I would be a young infant, and that she would still be breastfeeding me, but she was determined to make the trip to Baton Rouge for the dedication; she would take me in a basket with her—and she would take my sister, too. Although Betty was only three years old, Caroline hoped their bright little girl might remember the event; besides, she knew from all her psychology courses that she shouldn't leave the big sister home and take me along.

Because Long had been elected to the U.S. Senate, the dedication and the inaugural ceremony for the new governor, Oscar Allen, were held together, on May 16, 1932. The clouds hung heavy over the governor's mansion that morning as the officials gathered there for the parade. By the time the grand marshal, Colonel Seymour Weiss—not a relative—began to summon the marchers and lead the way to the capitol, a steady rain fell on the crowds already assembled in front of the State House.

Holding Betty on her lap, Caroline sat under a large umbrella waiting for the ceremonies to begin. From the first moments of the invocation through the rest of the inaugural speeches and music, she listened impatiently, waiting for the dedicatory ceremonies to begin. To make herself sit taller, Caroline rolled up her shawl and slipped it and her purse under her body so she could see Leon present the keys for the new capitol to Governor Allen. As Leon stood to deliver his speech, she held Betty high in her arms so that she could see above the heads of the people. Just as he began to speak, however, Betty proclaimed in a loud voice that she needed to go to the bathroom. Caroline groaned, but before she could move to take her, Betty was swept away by her grandmother, and the two of them missed the rest of the ceremony. Once the applause ended and Leon turned to take his seat, Caroline could see only the top of his head. She sat back in her chair and shivered with pride and exhilaration. She wanted to remember this moment always. After a few seconds, she got up from her seat, gazed once again through the rain in Leon's direction, and walked back to the hotel to join her children.

Despite some criticism over the cost to the state of $5 million and for the choice of the Fuller Company, an out-of-state firm, the thirty-four-story building created a sensation. "We have lived long but this is the noblest work of our whole lives": these first words spoken by Robert Livingston after he signed the Louisiana Purchase in 1803 are inscribed in huge letters in the stone façade of the capitol, and they echoed the sentiments of most people in the state. As Leon described it for the Baton Rouge *State Times* the afternoon of the dedication, "The massive base and towering shaft, loftiness growing out of broad solidity—suggests a duality of theme . . . the material resources of Louisiana and the historic struggles and achievements of her people, buttressing and sustaining the tower . . . the lofty aims and ambitions of sovereign people, guided and influenced by self-restraint and self-improvement to realization of higher and loftier spiritual values."

Leon at first concurred with those who had wanted a Louisiana contractor; he was satisfied, however, when the Fuller Company won, because he knew the company enjoyed experimenting with modern design while enriching its structures with classical elements. He was impressed with some of the company's previous works, especially the Flatiron Building on Fifth Avenue in New York, and the Lincoln Memorial and the National Cathedral in Washington, D.C. Leon knew Fuller's work and believed they'd work well together. Local contractors, however, were enraged; they vowed revenge. Leon was too enthralled with the details of the building to hear their oaths, which fell like dust in unattended rooms.

The capitol was the first structure to be completed in a multi-million-dollar building program for Louisiana. During the early half of the thirties, Weiss, Dreyfous and Seiferth planned and completed classroom and administrative halls, dormitories, a stadium and fieldhouse, a music and dramatic arts building, a library, and the president's house for the new LSU campus. On many occasions, they were invited back to Baton Rouge for special events.

In June, 1933, Caroline and Leon accompanied Lorado Taft to Baton Rouge to see Taft receive an honorary degree for his capitol sculptures. As special guests of James Smith, the president of the university, Caroline and Leon were invited to hear Taft's baccalaureate address. After the ceremony in the Greek theater, designed by Leon's firm, Caroline and Leon attended a reception at the Smiths' home. As they drove about the campus, Caroline looked with pride at the buildings Leon had designed, marveling at their splendor . . . but something brushed her senses, causing her to feel a sudden twinge of worry about him. Worry about what, she did not know. Maybe only that he'd been so frantically busy, or perhaps this unexplained anxiety was hormonal. She had felt changes in her body that she suspected were the early symptoms of another pregnancy. That must be it—not a premonition of some unknown issue, in spite of her uncanny intuition . . . for here were his monuments, and they were beautiful.

Throughout the early thirties, Leon and his partners saw many of these buildings rise. Under Long's direction and with Dr. Smith's supervision, the LSU campus grew during this time. In appreciation of his work, Leon was presented with an honorary doctorate of science at the LSU graduation ceremonies in April, 1935. Not wanting to leave the children, especially Leon, Jr., a very active one-year-old, Caroline and Leon drove up only for the ceremony and the reception in the garden of the Smiths' new home.

During this period, Leon and his partners traveled not only to Baton Rouge but also to other parishes in Louisiana as their work on public buildings continued and as they were more and more inundated with requests and contracts. They built a huge stadium in New Orleans' City Park, and soon after the capitol was completed, the firm designed a new, modern airport for the city. Located on an artificial spit of land jutting out into Lake Pontchartrain, the facility could accommodate both land and sea aircraft— at that time, an innovative concept. Because the land had been given to the state by Abe Shushan, the chairman of the levee board and one of Long's close associates, the airport was named in Shushan's honor. Once again, artists and sculptors were invited to create murals, friezes, and statues to adorn the main terminal's waiting room and the art deco façade, turning the airport into a showplace for Louisiana art—a temple dedicated to those giant "ships of the air," as Leon called them.

The largest, most challenging project placed before the firm, however, was Charity Hospital in New Orleans. A state-of-the-art public medical facility was another of Huey Long's "share the wealth" inspirations that he wanted Leon to bring to life. Once Leon had been chosen as the architect, meetings were held to approve the bonds. At one of these, a board member of Touro Infirmary, Elden Lazarus, fearing that the new hospital might overshadow Touro's prominence, decided to challenge Leon's expertise and ability to undertake this project rather than address the issues. After Lazarus finished his confrontational oration, Leon stood up and stated calmly, "You know, Mr. Lazarus, you chose me to build your house which, I believe, you are still living in." At that, the man sat down. No further opposition was heard, and Leon felt a deep sense of satisfaction. Caroline was pleased that Leon had demonstrated such self-control, despite his anger.

But this objection served as a portent, for the construction of Charity Hospital became one of the ingredients that Long opponents, seething with anger over other issues, were already beginning to pour into the cauldron. The general distrust of the Long administration sparked controversy over construction details, even though Leon and his partners engaged medical and engineering experts to attend to hospital requirements and structural questions. To plan the design and write the specifications for this modern hospital, they researched medical facilities and the latest in hospital technology and equipment; to augment their own expertise when planning operating rooms and other essentials, they worked closely with specialists. With its simple lines and art deco details, this immense white building became a landmark in downtown New Orleans. It was the tallest building yet to have been erected in this below-sea-level metropolis and was a massive structure for a city that was once a swamp. In the aftermath of Long's assassination and upheavals in the political scene, Charity Hospital would become part of the grand jury investigations. By the end of the thirties, the hospital had transformed itself into a huge white albatross that was hung around my father's neck.

But when it was completed, the hospital was applauded nationally for its functional design and modern features; in addition to efficiency, Leon also planned for artistic details, particularly the frieze above the main entrance, a large screen depicting life in Louisiana, carved by Enrique Alferez. On one of the panels in this screen, two sculptured ducks fly over the heads of some of the figures. Rique placed the ducks there for his own amusement, as a satirical comment on Louisiana politics. He was responding to Long's critics, who had been vocal in objecting to the administration's deducting money from the salaries of state employees and placing the unrecorded funds into a black cashbox for Huey's own use — one of Long's "innovations" that became an issue when the hospital was under construction, and was one of many instances of government corruption that began to hit the newspapers. Headlines and cartoons in the papers often made mention of Huey's infamous black box, called the deductions from salaries *de-ducks*, and blasted the Long administration for misusing taxpayers' money — funneling sums for personal or political purposes.

Rique may have been inspired by a cartoon that appeared on the editorial page of the *Times-Picayune* one morning, a drawing of ducks with dollar signs flying into the pockets of caricatures of Long and his associates. Not only was Rique attacking Long's corrupt administration when he molded these little ducks, his joke served also as personal vengeance aimed at Long. A few years earlier, in a French Quarter bar one night, Long had insulted Rique by uttering an ugly slur about Mexicans. Taking offense, Rique struck out at Long, but the next thing he saw was the floor coming up to his face. "His bodyguards had slipped me a Mickey Finn earlier," he told me. I wonder if Long ever noticed or understood the reason for Rique's ducks.

Huey Long's life ended when a bullet pierced his chest as he walked from the governor's office through his splendid capitol. Like Julius Caesar, he was assassinated on his way to the Senate, on Sunday, September 8, 1935. As Long crossed the great hall, a man hiding behind one of the pillars pulled a gun from under his coat and fired one shot. Long's bodyguards drew their guns and fired sixty-one bullets into the body of Dr. Carl Weiss (no relation to my father or to Seymour Weiss). During the next few days, as he lay on his hospital bed awaiting death, Long cried out, "Oh, Lord, don't let me die. I have a few more things to do. . . . My work for America is not finished."

Some of his goals may not have been reached, but his death roused people, already suspicious and angry, to attack Long and his methods. During his lifetime, Long was revered by his disciples, who saw him as a savior, even a messiah; others called him a demagogue, a dictator, and a tyrant. After his death, his name continued to provoke contention: some people loathed him for his tactics while others adored him for his ideology—his gospel, as my father called it. No one could remain neutral.

The marble wall in the ornate hall of the capitol, the setting for the dramatic climax to Huey Long's life, bears pockmarked witness to Long's bloody death, and the echoes of those gunshots rattled the state for the next decade. All the bitterness that had begun during Long's career never really ended. His enemies, having been silenced and outnumbered by those loyal to Huey or under his spell, arose and opened fire. Chaos and turmoil, like the aftermath of any bloody coup d'état, followed his death. Investigations and arrests led to humiliations, the smearing of names of anyone associated with the Kingfish and his years of political reign. In the aftermath of this discord, Huey Long's bronze figure stood brooding over his once-proud empire like Ozymandias, the tyrant in Shelley's poem whose fallen statue bears the inscription, "Look on my works, ye Mighty, and despair!" Long's statue quietly stands facing his capitol in the sunken garden designed by John Avery McIlhenny, Leon's friend, a horticulturalist, an ornithologist, and the inventor of Tabasco sauce.

Caroline and Leon had traveled to Highlands, North Carolina, in 1935, to spend a few weeks that summer at a mountain resort with their three children. Projects for the state buildings were incomplete, but Leon needed a few weeks away from the office, and he wanted time with his family. They hiked in the mountains and relished the cool mountain air so different from the humidity of New Orleans. Caroline and Leon had rejoiced when their son was born. Now that they had Leon, Jr., they felt their family was complete, and they wanted time alone with their three children.

Returning to the rustic main building for lunch after one of their morning hikes, they heard the radio blaring the news of Long's assassination. As Caroline and Leon listened, the reporters seemed uncertain about Long's condition, but as the afternoon passed, Leon knew Huey could not survive. It was over. Three days later, Long was dead. Once he heard the news, Leon's thoughts returned to the city. His happy, carefree summer ended.

The Long Hot Summer of 1939

Four years later, on an unseasonably hot day in June, 1939, Caroline and Leon sat quietly over their morning coffee. Even though the windows in the dining room were open, no breeze moved the muggy air, and these were the days before central air-conditioning in New Orleans. The children had gone outside with Nelly, the nurse, to splash in the wading pool, when Caroline and Leon heard the whistle of the newsboy as he rounded the corner and came up the walk between the azalea bushes. Leon went to get the paper, opened it to the front page, and slowly returned to the table. Caroline sat frozen as she read the headline that James Smith had mysteriously disappeared after being charged with embezzling money and construction materials that had been ordered for LSU buildings. The paper described his disappearance, his indictment and resignation . . . and more. Together Caroline and Leon read that the grand jury called to investigate corruption in Louisiana was also going to examine the records of Weiss, Dreyfous and Seiferth, architects for the buildings at LSU. Caroline grasped then that Leon—idealistic, imaginative, and probably a bit naïve and careless—had been beguiled: he had trusted and befriended the wrong men. She recalled the wave of worry, the twinge of fear that had touched her a few times over the years. But she never questioned his integrity.

As the weeks went by, the newspapers revealed stories of discrepancies in building costs, of materials embezzled and used for private homes, of furniture and millwork ordered but not used for the public buildings, and of "extras" paid for by the state and unaccounted for. Smith was traced to a hotel in Memphis, where he and his wife were registered as "Mr. and Mrs. Southern." Irate citizens formed a committee to demand his arrest, and a reward of $250 was posted for his return.

Smith, his wife, and his nephew were finally apprehended, arrested in Ontario, and shipped back to Baton Rouge, where Smith was placed in jail. All that month the grand jury continued its investigation, charging that Smith obtained bonds for the buildings without approval and used some of them as collateral for wheat market speculation. He and the contractors for the buildings, Caldwell and Hart, were charged with "financial irregularities," Governor Leche's words for their dealings. That same week, Governor Leche's name was linked with the scandals, forcing him to resign from office and move out of the governor's mansion. Until sentenced to prison, he retired to his summer home on the Tchefuncte River . . . near Kiskatom. The lieutenant governor, Earl Long—Huey's brother—took the oath of office and moved into the heavily guarded mansion.

On Sunday, June 26, rain began to fall early in the morning. By late afternoon, it became a deluge that flooded streets, stopped traffic, and blew down power lines; but with it came a break in the hottest weekend of the summer season. Two days later, Leon was subpoenaed to face the grand jury. Even though auditors had perused the office ledgers and had found no discrepancies, on August 1, he was formally charged with aiding and abetting crimes against the state in connection with the buildings he designed for LSU. From that point on, his name was associated with those already indicted, among them Smith, Seymour Weiss, Caldwell, and Monte Hart. The corruption in Louisiana, which someone called the "New Louisiana Purchase," began during Huey Long's reign and now had mushroomed. The grand jury investigations uncovered shady deals perpetrated by individuals within the highway commission, on the levee board, on the dock board, and in the department of conservation. The newspapers called it the Louisiana Hayride. Others called it a witch hunt and were alarmed at what they saw happening in Louisiana—people being presumed guilty without a fair hearing.

To shield the children from the publicity, Caroline and Ruth decided to drive the sixty-mile route across Lake Pontchartrain to Kiskatom, to spend the summer there. Leon assured Caroline, who wanted to stay with him, that he would be able to testify forthrightly, that the jury would believe that his office had played no part in these scandals. He could prove that he, personally, had not gained a cent above what he had earned honestly. He told her that his lawyer brother, Sol Weiss, would go to Baton Rouge with him, provide a bond for him, and convince the investigators of his innocence. Upon seeing Leon's picture plastered on page six of the morning *Times-Picayune,* and after hearing that same afternoon a newsboy riding his bike down Lowerline Street, rounding the corner of Dominican Street crying, "Extra, extra! Grand jury indicts Weiss," Caroline packed the car and left with the children.

Although her heart was torn in two, she watched the children swim, climb trees, and invent stories to perform in the attic theater. She remembered that just a few years earlier, while the house was under construction, I had noticed that the living-room ceiling created a raised section at one side of the attic and had exclaimed, "Oh, Daddy, that looks just like a stage!" Leon had promptly directed the carpenters to add steps and a proscenium with doors on either side. Leon had been charmed with our dramatic antics—especially our rendition of Hansel and Gretel abandoned in the dark forest.

This summer was the first but not the last retreat without Leon from the heat of the city. Caroline tried her best to keep her spirits up, amusing the children and trying to protect their innocence. Felix wrote supportive letters, and Ruth developed an annoying case of hives.

During all of August, the grand jury untangled threads of evidence, trying to tie Leon to the ring that had cheated the state. Some of those who had been close associates of Huey Long, such as Seymour Weiss and James Smith, were accused not only of "double dipping" with sales and contracts but also of income-tax irregularities and mail fraud. Because the tax charges, along with discrepancies found in disbursing WPA funds, were federal offenses, officials from Washington were summoned. Like a serial drama on the radio, each day's newspaper revealed intricate plots and additional characters involved in them. These stories aroused rage; readers called for revenge as they eagerly sought the details. After Abe Shushan, also implicated in the levee board scandals, went on trial for income-tax violations, the Shushan Airport, having been named originally in his honor, was renamed Lakefront Airport in his dishonor. Even though he was acquitted for tax evasion, crews were hired to remove Shushan's name from the front of the main terminal, and since all the doorknobs in the building contained his initials, every doorknob was replaced with a plain one. Leon saw a huge picture in the *Times-Picayune* of workmen swarming all over the building. He was shocked to read that while dismantling the Shushan name, these workmen discovered leaks and cracks in the building and claimed that cheap materials had been used instead of the copper flashing for the roof, as called for in the specifications. Caldwell and Hart were the contractors for this building as well as for all those built on the LSU campus while James Smith was president.

As the summer dragged on, the newspapers blasted Caldwell for fraudulent handling of funds. The front-page stories were based on grand jury disclosures that Caldwell had been the contractor for Leche Hall, the administration building at Louisiana Polytechnic Institute in northern Louisiana, which Weiss, Dreyfous and Seiferth had designed. As in the case of the LSU buildings for which Caldwell and Hart had been the contractors, the cost of that building exceeded the contract price by more than $86,000. When Leon went on trial several years later, he swore under oath before the jury that Governor Leche had approved that additional amount. Leche answered, as he had on other occasions in the past, that he couldn't recall having given his approval.

While Caroline remained across the lake with the children, Leon promised to telephone her to keep her informed about each day's story. Because the children, all under the age of ten, might be frightened if they learned what was happening to their father, Caroline didn't want the newspapers around; besides, the papers usually were a day late by the time they reached Madisonville, the little village three miles down the road. She was eager for the news, but neither she nor Leon wanted the children bruised by the emotions they both felt as they read or talked about what was happening. Late at night, after the children were asleep, Caroline waited at the telephone desk for the three loud rings on the ancient country phone that signaled their party line. Removing the receiver, she heard the sleepy voice of the Madisonville operator say, "Long distance calling from New Orleans, dawlin'." Caroline knew too well that all the phones on the same party line could listen in, along with the friendly operator who could double as local reporter. They tried to talk in code, sometimes even in French.

When she drove the five miles to Mandeville the next morning to buy groceries for the week, Caroline stopped by the post office to see if there were letters. She could see into the rented letter box before opening it, one envelope only. She sat down on a bench in front of the post office in the shade of an oak tree and looked at the familiar handwriting. It was an air-mail letter from her father, from Charlevoix. Shading her eyes from the glare of the sun on the white paper, she read his words several times: "Of course you know how much I sympathize with you and Leon in the action taken by the grand jury. There is no doubt in my mind that Leon was drawn into the Smith's mess innocently and that if the appearances or semblance of blame were used as a pretext for the prosecution, it is quite certain that [there] was no intent on his part to violate any statute. I can readily place myself in his position and would feel as keenly as he does that in an effort to help a friend who had befriended him his action was misconstrued and his intentions distorted to suit the purposes of his enemies. I wrote to George my opinion that the indictment would not hold and must on proper pleadings be dissolved or set aside." Caroline sat for a moment, then she tucked her father's letter in her purse, went to purchase some boiled crabs and a watermelon, and drove the five miles back to the children with confidence in her father's judgment.

By August 15, Caldwell was indicted for using the mails to defraud the university of more than $13,000 in kickbacks. Caldwell and Hart had been entrusted with obtaining bids for at least seven of the buildings in Baton Rouge; they were charged with adding the extras, which were returned to them in cash as kickbacks from subcontractors. In the next few weeks, Smith and Hart were convicted of mail fraud, with forty-two additional charges of fraud and embezzlement. At the end of August the grand jury recessed, and Caroline and the children returned to the city.

On Sunday, October 1, Leon got up early, dressed quietly, closed the door to the bedroom, and tiptoed downstairs. Caroline, always a light sleeper, followed. As Leon opened the front door to look for the morning paper, a blast of rain hit his face. He carried the wet paper to the dining room and unfolded it carefully. There on the front page glared the words that all night had troubled his sleep. They burned his eyes as he read that the Lincoln Parish grand jury in Ruston, Louisiana, had returned indictments of one to three counts against him, Julius, and Solis, along with Governor Leche and Monte Hart, for obtaining money under false pretenses in connection with the polytechnic institute building. According to the lengthy article in the newspaper, the cost of the building exceeded the bid by more than $27,000. A wave of fear washed over Leon as he saw in print that the first two counts could mean a maximum of five years' imprisonment and the third, a confidence-game charge, meant ten years. After he and Caroline both read the second page of the article, they sat and stared at each other, not able to speak. But that's ridiculous, he thought, I did not commit those crimes.

During the trials in the two years that followed, Leon continued to believe he could convince the judges and jury that he had not been part of these schemes, that he had not benefited from these deals. Leon also had faith that once Monte Hart knew he could not save himself, he would come forth and tell the truth, for he still believed that Monte was an honorable man. Then, Leon felt that he'd be cleared. Meanwhile, he decided, he'd take full responsibility as head of the firm. In that capacity, whatever occurred was his alone to face. He did not need Solis' or Julius' involvement, and for Caroline's father's sake, he wanted to protect Julius' name; Leon believed that like Don Quixote, he should battle his windmills alone. He trusted people and had no doubt that the system would judge him fairly. With abiding optimism and persuasive rhetoric, he nearly convinced Caroline that he would be exonerated. Although she believed in his innocence, privately she feared for him and worried about the horrible possible consequences. If men like Monte Hart commit larceny and cheat the state, what makes Leon believe, she wondered, in Hart's capacity or nobility to come forth with truth—and who would believe him? She tried to persuade herself that Hart had integrity. After all, he had always been respected as a contractor and member of the Uptown community—in fact, he lived on Audubon Boulevard, not far from Audubon Place, and was a neighbor of their cousins the Leon Cahns. Attempting to suppress her anxiety, she tried to share her husband's idealism and his faith in humanity.

The week before the trial was to begin, Leon came home from the office with the evening paper in his briefcase. Caroline had been sitting on the sofa in the living room trying to read a novel she had begun a few weeks earlier. The room seemed unusually quiet, but the laughter of the children playing drifted downstairs, and from the kitchen she heard the new cook, Eula, humming as she prepared grillades for dinner. When Caroline saw his drawn face, the book dropped on the floor as she went to greet him. "What's wrong?" she managed to inquire, feeling a tightening in her abdomen even though she tried to control her panic. He took her arm, led her into the solarium, and closed the door.

"Hart's dead," he said in a monotone. "They found him dead this morning . . . on the tile floor. . . . He went downstairs to the taproom of his house and shot himself in the head."

Leon had worked closely with Hart while the LSU buildings were under construction. Their relationship had been one of mutual respect and cordiality, for Leon liked and trusted the man. In fact, when Hart needed capital for a stumbling business deal he was involved in, he had asked Leon to help by buying some shares. That was when Leon became part owner of a dairy farm, The Southern Dairy, located a few miles up River Road from New Orleans. He and Caroline enjoyed taking the children to the farm. Wandering through the barns watching the milking of the cows, picnicking under one of the oldest and largest live oaks in Louisiana, the President, and climbing the levee to see the ships on the river steaming to New Orleans became a favorite Sunday outing. His involvement in that deal also became an issue during the investigations. Yes, Leon was always helping people— trusting people was his nature. Hart's death felt like a double blow to Leon: he had judged Hart a friend, and he believed that this friend could rescue him.

Throughout the long years of trials, Leon pleaded innocent, claiming that he had been taken advantage of by contractors, but the jury found him guilty. They didn't believe him, his witnesses, or his attorney, Hugh Wilkinson—probably an unfortunate choice to plead for his innocence, because Wilkinson was a former law partner of Huey Long. People Leon had worked with, such as John Edgeworth, came to his defense as witness to his innocence. All of them spoke about his integrity, his talent, and his past record of honesty and fairness to people, but the evidence brought out against him by those outraged by the corruption in the state during Long's administration swayed the jury. More records were seized, linking Leon to the deals that the others had been engaged in.

The final blow had to do with structural problems found in the Charity Hospital building. Even though engineers with nationally known reputations as foundation experts judged that the cracks in the building were the normal settling of a large building, especially one constructed in a city below sea level, minds were set against him. Those testifying against him claimed that the piles used to support the building were cut off before they had been driven completely into the ground. According to expert witnesses for the defense, however, the piles had been driven as deep into the earth as called for in the specifications: the contract stated that after driving the piles as far as possible, if three additional blows would send the piles no deeper, no further hits would be used; the engineers asserted that at that point, the piles must be resting on solid rock.

There were other charges in connection with the hospital: papers showed a photograph of Leon and Huey Long watching a huge building being moved out of the way of the construction of Charity Hospital. The picture was taken originally because moving this large structure was deemed an engineering feat—one that skeptics had declared could not be done. When, however, the site of the hospital was changed, the building was moved back to its original place. The *Times-Picayune* printed the same photograph, only this time it was used to establish Leon's connection to Long and the corrupt building practices of Long's administration. Because Leon had been the architect for all of the projects in question, the jury was convinced that he was involved in the corruption. Despite testimony by other contractors and despite Leon's spotless reputation, the overwhelming evidence against him seemed more tangible to the jury than did all the words of friends and associates. He was convicted of mail fraud—a federal crime—since he had mailed an architect's certificate requesting payment for higher costs during the construction of the building at Ruston. Governor Leche still refused to acknowledge that he had authorized the additional charges. I had always wondered why Mother and Daddy were never friendly with Leche. Even though his summer house was next door to Kiskatom and he once gave me a stuffed baby alligator when we stopped our boat at his dock, we never visited again.

Caroline was devastated, but she summoned her courage and channeled her energies into helping him. She attempted to find among his papers evidence that could be used to support him when the case went to a higher court. Using an ancient office typewriter that refused to print several characters and skipped extra spaces, she appealed to architects, contractors, officials, lawyers, judges, friends, and associates—anyone she could think of who might come to his defense. "This man," she wrote, "has had disgrace heaped upon him because he was before a court and jury who do not even understand what an architect is and does. . . . A crooked regime used the trusting nature of this man as an unsuspecting tool to cover up overcharges. . . . Here in his own community everyone has confidence in his honesty and ability. I have written proof of this."

Her pleas knocked feebly at closed doors. It did not matter. Leon was denied a new trial even though some people—even one of the three judges—argued for a mistrial. Some even compared the case to the Dreyfus Affair in France, since Leon was Jewish. Like Dreyfus, Leon had achieved considerable success in spite of being Jewish, which would make him a convenient scapegoat for jealous, vengeful people—an angry mob looking for someone on whom to unleash the rage and fix the blame for all the corruption Long left in his wake.

Others called it a witch hunt because of the virulent anti-Long fury that swept through the state, particularly in north Louisiana, which was Ku Klux Klan territory and the setting for the trial. A racist juror might not deal justly with a man named Weiss—especially one closely associated with Huey Long, for Long was an enemy of the Klan. Moreover, some people might have identified Leon Weiss with two other Jewish associates of Long—Abe Shushan and Seymour Weiss, who had just been convicted of embezzlement. Conspiracy had been one of the charges.

In the appeals that followed, Leon was denied a retrial, even though new evidence had been introduced, in particular, a cashier's check that he had endorsed; but the rules of evidence prevailed: the jury was instructed to view with limited vision this new exhibit placed before them. Even though the check might further prejudice the jury against Leon, two of the three judges allowed it to be used. The third judge dissented, arguing against using a new exhibit, something that had not been part of the trial. This important piece of evidence—the check—Mother explained, had been an error on the part of the office bookkeeper, who found his mistake after Leon had endorsed the check and given it to Dr. Smith. Instead of asking for it back, Leon trusted that Dr. Smith would tear it up as he promised, but Smith used it for one of his illegal investments, which of course implicated Leon.

Following the verdict and the appeal, at the fifth circuit court of appeals in September, 1941, Leon was sentenced to five years in federal prison for use of the mails to defraud the state. But before he served his term, the judges met once again to argue the issue of further appeals.

While the three judges deliberated, Caroline and Leon waited in their hotel room. There was still a chance, they hoped. This optimism had sustained them, or perhaps in supporting each other, Caroline and Leon became a separate keystone that refused to let go and to give way as the heavy weight of those days heaped upon them. Despite the fury of the crowds, the vengeful witnesses (especially the contractors still angry at not having been awarded the capitol contract), and the incriminating evidence stacked high against them during the trials and the appeals, Caroline and Leon had preserved their faith in the system and their belief in justice. Throughout the long days of listening to sworn testimony and watching the drama unfold in the courtroom, they had felt certain the jury would act without bias. And even at the end of the trial, when they heard the verdict, the word *guilty* didn't seem real. The voices in the room seemed muffled, as if Caroline and Leon were under water and the source of these words were far above them. The entire courtroom scene blurred, taking on a dreamlike aura. Dazed, they drifted out of the courtroom to their hotel room, feeling numb, weary, and alone; but until the judges could come to a decision about whether the case would be heard at a higher level, the bail bond would keep Leon free.

And now, as they waited in the dusk of late afternoon, the sun cast eerie shadows on the yellow walls of the room, and rays bounced off Caroline's wedding ring, breaking into rainbow speckles that played with the murmuring ceiling fan. Although the fan purred softly, the room felt steamy, and the air smelled of stale smoke from the unwashed ashtray on the night table next to the bed, but they were too tired to care. The room was warm, yet Caroline felt chilled as she stood by the desk chair and watched Leon take his wallet and change from his pants pockets, place them on the night table, remove his shoes, loosen his tie, and lie across the bed on top of the musty bedspread. Caroline thought she should call home to check on the children, but there was no phone in the room, so she took a piece of stationery from the desk drawer and sat down to write instead.

Just as she positioned the pen to begin, a knock startled them both to their feet. Caroline started for the door, but before she could move, Leon gently held her back. He slipped into his shoes, walked to the door, and loosened the chain that held it fast. Once he had turned the knob releasing the lock, the door pushed open against him, and before he could step back, two burly figures in blue crossed the threshold into the room. Without a word and without time for Leon to say goodbye, the two policemen grabbed him and led him roughly from the room. Two out of the three judges had ruled against him. No longer free on bail, he was taken away.

Caroline stood frozen ... wanting to run after him ... unable even to utter a sound. Staring at the open door ... fixing the sight. Not real. Not real. Stuffing clothes into the two suitcases, she somehow found her way to the train and journeyed the long way home alone.

5
The War Years

*I*n my preteen years, while Daddy was away, I tried to ignore his absence. It was difficult, but I was preoccupied by adolescent concerns: petty jealousies over girlfriends, fantasizing over boys, and adapting to changes in my body. Other than my own fragmented memories of Mother reading letters from him and missing her when she went to Atlanta to visit him in the federal penitentiary each month, those twenty months he spent in prison are still a blank to me, except the strong memory of worrying what people knew and, if so, what they thought or said to one another. My friends never asked me any questions, and I confided in no one. I missed him, and the time he was away seemed like an eternity—a hollow space carved out of my life.

Time seemed to move slowly. Even the familiar road to Kiskatom seemed to go on forever; but that may have been because of the war: Mother never drove faster than thirty miles an hour to save gas, for rationing limited our supply, and she believed it was patriotic not to exceed the prescribed speed. I hated the drive home on Sundays, even though listening to Jack Benny and Fibber McGee on the radio made us laugh—especially the crashing sounds when that closet door opened and all the clutter fell out. During the summer months at Kiskatom, when the heat of midday kept us indoors, we sat reading on the screened porch that wrapped around the living room. Or to be patriotic, we kept busy knitting squares to give to the Red Cross, for someone to sew into blankets. We also helped by carefully peeling tin foil from chewing-gum wrappers and rolling it into balls for bullets, and we mixed yellow food coloring with white oleo to make it look like butter. Evenings, we listened to the Quiz Kids, the Andrews sisters, and the Hit Parade. Best friends sometimes visited for long weekends, but we no longer played host to Daddy and Mother's crowd, who used to come and fill the house with laughter. And since Daddy wasn't there to roast hot dogs, we had no more picnics under the oak trees for sailors stationed at a nearby navy base; we had entertained these young men on several occasions during the early years of the war, and they had brought us Hershey bars from the commissary because the bars were rationed and we couldn't buy any.

Mother has told me little about visiting Daddy or what he experienced while in prison, except that she had to sit behind the screen when they talked. She told me he taught reading and writing to other inmates and listened to war news on the radio. There was nothing more she wanted to tell me about those days. She declared in a curt voice, "You know what it's like. . . . You've seen movies . . . how people talk through a grille." We had journeyed as far as she wanted to take me through the silences.

I can't remember anything about the day he returned, only the throb of anticipation I held privately inside me all that school day. I do know that when he returned after serving less than two years of his five-year sentence, he seemed different to me, older and distant somehow. He looked and acted tired, I thought; but my world had moved outside, away from him, since I had plunged into a self-absorbed sphere of adolescence.

In a blue mood one Sunday following dinner at my grandfather's house, I left the table and went outside to sit and mope on one of the big wicker rocking chairs on the front veranda while the adults finished their coffee. When Daddy came out, I followed him to the car. I wanted to get home to the telephone and call my friend Peggy; we had been in the middle of a Monopoly game when I had to leave for Sunday dinner. Daddy stopped me before I had opened the car door and asked me to go back and kiss my grandfather. When I groaned and refused, he raised his arm above his head and hit me—a terrible blow to my face that staggered me, as I remember. All the years of my life he had never hit me or even raised his voice at me. I ran from him—I wanted to run away from the humiliation and the shock that I felt. I couldn't comprehend what made him so furious at me. I don't remember going back to kiss my grandfather, but I must have. The sting of that blow and the pain of humiliation never left me, but I think I understand his misplaced temper and why my not kissing my grandfather goodbye enraged my father: he could not bear having hurt Mother, and he hated feeling diminished in Felix's eyes. After all of Leon's efforts to prove himself worthy of her, he felt his success had slipped away. Despite having kept Julius out of the ordeal, Leon knew his disgrace had stained Caroline's family's name. Although most people, including Felix, believed in his innocence and were convinced that he had been a victim of political persecution, his imprisonment had mortified him and shattered all he had gained. Leon felt that he had worked hard to earn a place in the family and that Felix had finally accepted him and had been proud of the firm's achievements. He believed Felix had trusted him, never doubted him, and now, paradoxically, Leon found himself in the loathsome position of being financially obligated to Felix, who had paid legal fees, bonds, and fines—a place my father had never wanted to be in. With that slap, I paid the heavy price of Daddy's remorse.

Sitting on a chair next to Mother, I looked at her face, but I could detect no expression of suffering around her eyes and mouth as she shared these slivers of her long-hidden story. At the hard places we arrived at in our dialogue, the pauses became longer and the silences difficult to break, particularly after she told me about his being taken away. After that, we sat quietly for a long while. I could hear the hum of the vacuum cleaner downstairs and the rattle of pots and pans in the kitchen. But without any prompting, Mother began again.

"When he came back it wasn't long before he had big jobs. He started right up again. I call it his resurrection. People believed in him and wanted him to design their buildings. For a while he worked alone, then with Arthur Davis, and finally with Eddie Silverstein. Eddie was a peach. He was Leon's cousin, you know. They were partners until Leon died. Arthur and Eddie knew Leon was treated unfairly. They believed he had been a victim. Most people did. The worst was that the architects' association threw him out . . . and he founded the Louisiana chapter. There's a plaque from them in the other room. . . . And Julius and Solis refused to take him back—they threw him out, too. Leon said they'd last no longer than a couple of years without him." She uttered a rueful laugh. "He was right. That's all they did."

"His biggest job was the Jung Hotel. You know he remodeled it and built a huge addition . . . an almost \$3 million contract. I helped him with decorating some of the meeting rooms . . . just like before. It was finished just before he died. It was his last project. That's why you were married in the Cotillion Room in the new Jung Hotel. I was so proud of it—that room with all the flowers. It was so beautiful. Do you remember?"

All that I could think about or marvel at was how she could muster the strength to plan a wedding that would follow only three months after her husband's death. But in spite of what she said, I thought that Daddy had changed after prison. He seemed not to have his same spirit.

I looked at her and tried to envision how my mother endured those trying years. I wondered how, while Daddy was away, she was able to wake up, face each day, greet other people, and check her anger or self-pity. Sitting beside her now, I tried to ask her how she managed such control, for I never heard her complain or utter any sound of grief or loneliness, but she did not respond. I remember that once I saw her sitting alone in her dimly lit bedroom holding a letter from Daddy, but I never saw her cry. Nor was she ever impatient or sharp with us. She rarely talked about Daddy when he was away, nor did she ever tell us much about what happened, except to say, "Daddy made a mistake."

We asked no questions. The wall of silence with its façade of serenity was erected to protect us, as if not mentioning Daddy's tragedy made it unreal. Perhaps Mother imagined, like Jay Gatsby, that by erasing the past, she could blot out the years Daddy was in prison and could obliterate the tragedy of his fall. Maybe, like Gatsby, Mother believed in a green light as a beacon to navigate toward: she and Daddy buried those terrible years they experienced just as they had buried in profound silence the death of Daddy's other child so many years before. Like the green light, the lamp in the cupola of the capitol inspired them to look upward and outward, not back or down; for its light radiated from a monument that symbolized Daddy's idealism, spirituality, and love of beauty. Daddy believed that he was building "forever," not for "present delight nor for present use alone." He had written, "Let it be such work as our descendants will thank us for, and let us think as we lay stone on stone that a time is to come when those stones will be held sacred because our hands have touched them, and that men will say as they look upon the labor and wrought substance of them, '*See*, this our fathers did for us.'"

In a rowboat on the bayou at Kiskatom. Top to bottom: Daddy, Ruth, me, Mrs. Levy, Helen Seiferth, Mr. Levy (an architect from New York), Mother, and Betty, holding an alligator given to us by Governor Leche

The three Weiss children at Kiskatom, *ca.* 1938: Bubby, me, and Betty

"Big House" at Kiskatom

Mother (Caroline Dreyfous) in Charlevoix, Michigan,
in July of 1927, the summer before her marriage to Leon

Caroline Dreyfous, probably that same summer

Daddy (Leon Weiss) in his World War I uniform

Caroline's wedding portrait, September 29, 1927

Leon Weiss in the summer of 1927

The Dominican Street home of Leon and Caroline, where I grew up

Portions of the Drysdale murals in our Dominican Street dining room

Leon Weiss and Attilio Piccirilli, sculptor for the new state capitol

The new Louisiana state capitol, designed by Weiss, Dreyfous, & Seiferth, 1932

Mother at her grandmother Carrie Seeman's home
in Cincinnati, with Betty and me

"Unk" George Abel Dreyfous

My portrait at thirteen, about the time I tried to talk to Unk about Daddy

The Roman candy wagon, on St. Charles Avenue

My two grandfathers, Theodore Weiss (left) and Felix Dreyfous (right),
with Betty in the carriage

Ruth Dreyfous

My maternal grandparents, Julia and Felix Dreyfous

Daddy's mother, Lena Silverstein Weiss

My maternal great-grandparents, Caroline and Abel Kaufman Dreyfous

Abel and Caroline's house on Esplanade Avenue

Felix and Julia's home on Jackson Avenue, the birthplace of Caroline and Ruth

The Dreyfous home on Audubon Place, designed by Uncle Julius

Mother on her ninetieth birthday

Alby and me with our children and grandchildren

*I*nterlude

Travel itself is part of some longer continuity.

—Eudora Welty

*N*ow when I journey home to New Orleans, before Mother awakens and has breakfast, I start my days with a jog around Audubon Park, along the road now reserved for bikers, skaters, runners, and walkers instead of automobiles.

As I walked down the path from the front steps of Mother's house to the street on the first day after arriving in February a few years ago, beads of dew glistened in the early morning sunlight on the grass and on the buds of awakening daffodils, but the air felt crisp on my bare arms, and I shivered as I glanced back at the shuttered windows of Mother's room.

My route took me first down Dominican Street, past the old Dominican convent with its white balconies, colonnades, and oak-sheltered cloister. Nuns in black habit no longer meditate along the paths: since the convent has been converted into a law school, Loyola University law students' bicycles now grace the balconies where nuns once walked. Despite minor alterations, the façades of the old buildings seem to have memorized their previous uses, standing there facing St. Charles Avenue like celibate ghosts, as a reminder of less frantic times.

After passing the back of the buildings, I followed Dominican Street until its end on Walnut Street. I thought back to the days I used to ride my bike on Dominican Street before it was paved, when mud puddles ruined our shoes and deep ditches swallowed our softballs, when an open-sided garbage wagon pulled by mules—we called it the "perfume wagon"—clattered down the bumpy road each morning, as did a horse-drawn cart laden with fruit and fresh vegetables. From his seat on front of the cart, an old Cajun farmer cried out his products. I loved to hear his melodic drawl—"black bey—rees . . . straw bey—rees . . . ,"—as I awakened in my room in the morning to the sound of his song and the rattle of the wagon wheels. At night, we heard the droning wail of trains on the levee and the moan of tugboats pulling barges on the Mississippi just a few blocks away. If the wind blew from that direction, we could sometimes hear the roar of the lions in the zoo: an eerie sound for city ears and sometimes a scary one in winter as we lay in bed in our darkened room. We used to cover our heads with our blankets to protect ourselves, just as we pulled our sheets over our heads to defend ourselves from mosquitoes in the summertime. Dominican Street seemed like a country road then, with its open ditches and muddy pools; it was not like the paved one I now run on when I come home to New Orleans.

After crossing Walnut Street, I entered the park near the golf course, right across from the gray stucco apartment building Mother and Daddy lived in during their first year of marriage. Daddy's father, Theodore, lived in this building with them until he died in 1929; and my sister, Betty, was born there. Soon after her birth, they built the house just down Dominican Street, where I was born, where my mother still lives, that brick house hidden from the street by giant azalea bushes and crape myrtles. On this winter day, pink azalea blossoms adorned the branches, but the crape myrtles' pruned tops would wait until summer to burst into their rosy bloom. My route through the park took me first to the grove of live oak trees whose moss-tressed limbs turn the path into a shady arched nave. At that time of morning, as I jogged along, I was greeted by young mothers pushing baby strollers and by robins, squirrels, mockingbirds, and other runners. I like the shade of those trees and the mottled shadows they cast on the path in front of my feet as I run.

Leaving the oaks, I approached the Magazine Street side of the park and gazed across the street at the entrance to the zoo and the sad ruins of the public swimming pool and bathhouses. We were never allowed to swim there for fear of polio and the other dread diseases children died from in the thirties and forties. Some summers, during severe epidemics, to check the spread of the disease, the pool was closed by the city health department. After the civil rights movement ended segregation, the gates of the pool were shut because of a different fear: rather than let the pool be integrated, city officials closed it down, leaving it to the weeds, grasses, and nesting birds. Although it reopened for a while as a neighborhood facility and bore the proud name the Whitney M. Young Memorial Pool, it never looked cared for. Now it is closed once again, probably for economic or political reasons this time. Most white parents had abandoned it, just as they had forsaken the neighborhood schools in the early sixties—sending their children to the newly opened all-white academies. When I pass by Audubon School on my way to the park, I see mostly black children playing ball on the cement, climbing the rusted jungle gym, and swinging on the unpainted swings where once only white children played.

I had moved away from the South when Audubon Zoo was first opened to blacks. Once the laws changed, my aunt Mathilde took Sylvia, her cook, for her first visit to the zoo. Mathilde told us that when Sylvia saw giraffes swinging their long necks as they ran, she screamed with delighted laughter and disbelief. Before that day, even though she had lived in the city all her life, she had never been allowed to see zebras, elephants, or giraffes. I can imagine her wonder at the live animals she had seen before only in books.

Yes, the zoo has always been a favorite place. We liked to hear the sea lions splash and bark when the keeper called them by name as he tossed each in turn a large whole fish. I used to love to watch the elephants eat our peanuts, and I laughed and jumped away when the monkeys spit water at us, probably because they were kept in crowded dirty cages, but I did not know that then. Many things eluded me when I was a child growing up on Dominican Street, or I never thought to question them. On some days when I played alone behind the white picket fence surrounding our yard, between the slats I could see dark-skinned children with red and yellow ribbons in their hair passing by on their way home. They were our neighbors, who lived two blocks down on Millaudon Street, toward the river, in unpainted two-family cottages jammed so close to each other that the children had no yard to play in. Built without halls, these houses contain four or five rooms connected in a row from the front door to the rear. The long, skinny structures are called "shotgun houses": if someone shot a gun through the house, the bullet would fly right through all the rooms and out the back door.

I don't remember asking why these children who passed my house every day were not invited in or the reason I was not supposed to talk to them. No one ever told me not to, but for some reason I thought I shouldn't. I wonder if I ever asked why the movable signs saying FOR COLORED PEOPLE ONLY prohibited me from sitting in the back of the streetcar, or why colored people used separate doors directing them upstairs to the balconies of movie theaters. I didn't understand then the significance of the sign on the door of the laundromat near my school that stated in bold letters COLORED PEOPLE IN WHITE UNIFORMS ONLY. I noticed with curiosity the segregated society I lived in—the separate drinking fountains, toilets, train-station waiting rooms, and even the dishes in our home. These images certainly impressed me because they have rested unresolved in my memory all these years, but at the time I lacked the capacity to challenge or criticize. I accepted everything without questioning, for I believed in the absolute wisdom of the adult world. I saw strange inconsistencies such as our having only white nurses caring for us as infants and black cooks preparing our food, but I could not comprehend the assumptions or the dreadful fears and beliefs underlying the ugly realities of segregation or the racist language I heard all around me and used myself. For I was brought up to be a passive child, a silent little girl.

Our neighborhood, like most in Uptown New Orleans, was a conglomerate of rich and poor, white and black, Jew and Gentile. There were no Jewish sections of the city. Unlike other cities, in Uptown New Orleans wealthy white people lived in large houses with fenced-in gardens, surrounded by clusters of poorer white or black families living in apartments, cottages, and duplexes. Until about fifth or sixth grade, when we played softball on the street with neighborhood kids, I didn't know any of the children nearby, except for my best friend, Peggy Burkenroad, who lived across the street, and John and Tommy Godchaux, whose house was around the corner. Playmates—even Peggy—came with their nurses to play in our backyard. Their parents belonged to the same social circle as mine, which meant that they probably had attended the same schools, were members of the Reform Temple Sinai, could track their family background several generations back to Germany or France, and had remained friends for several generations . . . but I wasn't cognizant of any kind of discrimination or segregation at that stage of my life. I barely knew there was another world outside my garden walls.

I think I may have associated this protection from neighborhood children with the threat of germs. Somehow these notions became confused in my thoughts and responses, but at age ten I fell in love with the boy across the street, Tommy Eagan, who one day convinced me that I should let him kiss me as we sat hidden by bushes in the backyard. I was not aware that he was Catholic—not until he became ill with rheumatic fever and a crucifix over his bed glared down at me when I stole across the street to visit him. Despite the fear of germs and illness implanted in me, I had to see him: somehow, even though I was only twelve at that time, I must have sensed that he was dying. I was shocked when he pointed to the bedside table laden with pills and confessed that at times he thought of gulping the whole lot of them and ending it all. When he told me Margot Bouden had visited him in the hospital and asked me why I hadn't come, my excuse about Mother's worry about germs sounded pathetic to me; his rueful laugh appalled me. Of course, I never told Mother, but I must have suffered terrible guilt over my impulsive breaking of the boundaries. I never saw him again, for not long after my visit, I heard that he had died.

He was my first and last Christian romance and the only neighbor I remember. Once I went to school, my circle widened, but I was still insulated, now behind the bricks of a private school for privileged children, Jewish and Christian. At Isidore Newman School, founded as a manual training school by a Jewish philanthropist to educate the orphans from the Jewish Children's Home, the majority of my classmates were Gentiles, but in elementary school, I did not know the significance of religious differences and only a trickle of children came from the Jewish Home. Since I never attended Sunday school because Daddy and Mother took us across the lake to Kiskatom every weekend instead, I had no clear picture of what being Jewish meant. My Jewish friends probably didn't know much more than I did about Judaism, even though some of them went to Sunday school. They learned about the prophets and about biblical events, but the lessons did not include Jewish culture or traditions, and they did not learn any Hebrew—except to memorize and pronounce slowly the transliteration of a few lines in the prayer book in praise of God: *Shemah Yisroel, Adonoi Eloh-einu, Adonoi, Echad . . .* or *Baruh Atah Adonoi. . . .*

Because we did not follow any Jewish rituals or customs, we believed we were like everyone else—particularly since we celebrated Christmas with a tree, as did all of my Jewish friends, and we all joined in when carols were part of school programs, unaware that these were Christian songs. To emphasize the secular nature of Christmas, we put an angel on the top of our tree instead of a star, believing the tree would then have no Christian symbolism. Once a guest recognized the angel's face, which we had clipped from the bridal page of the newspaper and pasted on the head of our homemade angel.

Like everyone else in our class, on Easter morning we hunted for our baskets of eggs and ate ham for Sunday dinner, never connecting Easter with Christ. Since all my friends celebrated Christian holidays and not Jewish ones, we assumed Jews everywhere observed Christmas and Easter as we did. We had no idea that other Jewish families refused to sing carols and celebrated Hanukkah instead of Christmas. Since we were southerners, our culture and our beliefs reflected a long history of living in the South. We ate red beans and rice (stewed with the leftover ham bone) for lunch on Saturday, feasted on raw oysters or river shrimp on special occasions, and never heard of bagels and lox. No one I knew attended services on the Sabbath except when required to for confirmation year. Since I lacked any knowledge of the difference between Christians and Jews when I was in second grade, I asked Mother if I could have a gold cross to wear on a chain, like some of my friends. I remember being told that Jewish girls did not wear gold crosses, but I was not told why. Until I went to a Jewish camp in Maine and met new friends from Manhattan and Philadelphia, I had no idea that Jews had special foods and rituals and could not eat boiled crabs, bacon, or oyster pie. In fact, my friends tell me it's now a standing joke that the recipe for making matzo balls in New Orleans begins with frying onions in bacon grease.

My first experience with Jewish customs was during high school, when Cynthia Miller and I became friends. We walked to her house from school on Fridays, and when we went into her kitchen for milk and cookies, I watched with amazement as her grandmother set out candles in preparation for the sabbath. Cynthia had to explain to me all the Friday night sabbath rituals and rules. When she told me her grandmother spoke Yiddish, I was surprised to learn that there was a special language Jews spoke. I remember feeling that something was missing in my upbringing, but I didn't have any notion of what it was—only that I liked the warmth and intimacy I felt in this traditional Jewish home. I think it may have been at this time that I decided to stay weekends at my aunt Ruth's house on Audubon Place so that I could attend Sunday school and be confirmed. I suppose I must have felt a need for religion and prayer, or perhaps I felt excluded from social activities associated with the temple, but in either case I enrolled in Sunday school. My parents thought that I only wanted to get all those confirmation gifts of costume jewelry, stationery, and perfume from their friends, but as I reflect on it now, I think I missed religion in my life.

I don't remember when I became aware that some of my friends got together on Friday nights without the small number of us who were Jewish. On weekends in eighth and ninth grades, these girlfriends splintered off to attend dances (with other girls from Miss McGehee's, an elite private school). They were invited to dances called the "Eight O'Clocks" during eighth grade and the "Nine O'Clocks" the next year in preparation for their coming out, and we went to our own dancing school in some woman's living room on Soniat Street. Throughout high school, we went our divided ways at parties on weekends, though we remained friends during the week. Never expecting to be included in their social events, we accepted the separation, believing it was correct, for some unknown reason. Since no Jewish girl was invited to any of the dances, none of us felt left out; besides, we believed it was right because that was the way it always had been, and we trusted in traditions. I did have crushes from time to time on non-Jewish boys in my class, especially Bruce Burglass, but I never expected he'd ask me out. When to my great delight I was elected cheerleader my senior year (for my agility and not my good looks), I was one of the first Jewish girls selected, and I fantasized about going steady with a football or basketball hero, but that never happened except for a time with Ivan Victor; he was Jewish, however. Aunt Ruth told me when she was growing up in New Orleans, the situation was the same: she was part of the "inner circle," except when events included boys. Then no Jewish girls were invited.

I don't recall thinking that we were being discriminated against or that the cause was anti-Semitism, for "Semitic" had nothing to do with any of us. We didn't see ourselves looking or acting differently from Christians; to us, Orthodox Jews were the ones who were distinctive. We were too naïve to recognize that the adult world was dividing us and depriving us of our freedom to choose our friends.

I glanced once more at the new entrance to the zoo as I continued on my run through the park. I thought about all that's changed since I lived here long ago—and yet how much has stayed the same. The courts have mandated integration and freedom, but boundaries still exist. In Audubon Park, the animals no longer are kept in small cages; the zoo has been renamed the zoological gardens, and zebras and antelopes roam freely on simulated natural landscapes surrounded by moats and fences. The zoo is now open to everyone. Both Sylvia and Mathilde died just a few years ago, and I journey back to the South only for short visits.

As I continued my jog around the circular road in the park, my course took me along the muddy lagoon where I smiled at a Canada goose, wondering if he also had flown down from Connecticut and felt displaced, sharing the same lagoon with a Louisiana heron.

I could see the gothic tower of Holy Name Cathedral peering above the trees as I left the waterfowl and neared the St. Charles Avenue side of the park. On this last quarter mile of the path, two blond students, having crossed between the automobiles and streetcars, jogged into the park through the tall, concrete gateposts and easily passed me by. I finished the circle, left the park, and hurried home to have breakfast with Alby. Since Parkinson's disease slows him down, he had just finished dressing when I returned. By that time, Mother was waiting for me to join her in her bedroom for a mug of New Orleans coffee, brewed so thick and black that we called it "Mississippi River mud."

Mother, Alby, and I chattered away until lunchtime, when we tested the February sun by eating boiled crabs and crawfish outside on the terrace in view of Mother's garden with its mammoth camellia trees, elephant ears, jasmine vine, sweet-olive tree, and bird-bath fountain designed by Alferez. We broke apart the shells of the crabs to pick and eat the spicy morsels, cooling the peppery burning of our mouths and lips with sips of Dixie beer. We ate until the crab juices ran down to our elbows, which meant we had to stop—a crab-eating rule Daddy made years ago.

As we ate, I watched a squirrel climb the trunk of the oak tree, scamper out over one huge limb, leap to the Japanese plum tree, and climb down the fragile branches of the paper-white bushes that grow against the brick wall at the back of the garden. Mother wore her flowered housecoat and sported the straw hat decorated with yellow paper flowers that her companion, Rosie, had made for her. She sat in a wrought-iron chair shored up with pillows, savoring the crab and memories of different seasons in the garden when her family was growing, when we played on the swings and slide that used to be in the back play yard before it was sold for building lots and closed off by the brick wall. That was after Daddy died and I moved away.

But during the years that I lived here, I spent endless sunny days beyond that brick wall, enclosed by thick bushes and chain-link fences, protected from the outside world. Denied access to adult concerns, Betty, Bubby, and I were sent out to play on our slide and swings, away from the worries Mother dealt with indoors. Looking at her today, I wondered how she stood the ordeal of Daddy's trial and his incarceration without talking about it to anyone. But just as women survived nine months without mentioning the word *pregnant*, hiding their heavy bodies behind loose garments or even staying indoors, Mother bore her fear for my father and her pain when he was away without mentioning its name. I don't know what she did with the anger she must have felt, for I never saw it, and I never saw her cry. Perhaps from her French and German Jewish roots she inherited her stoicism; she was expected never to show emotion, for that would be seen as weakness: outward displays of feeling seemed not to be a family trait. "I never cry," she told me, "and Leon taught me not to worry about things we could not change. 'What is without remedy must be without regard,' he used to say." After a moment's silence, she added, "You know very well that nothing's fixed by thinking about it or crying over it . . . but your burden—Alby's illness—is God's dealing, and mine was done by human devils."

Since we were sheltered from all conversations that might have occurred between Mother and Daddy when we were children, and because she did not express her sorrow to us, we all grieved silently and separately, never mentioning to each other that we missed our father. I know that I nurtured feelings that longed to break out of the tight little buds that held them, but talking about his being in prison seemed forbidden, obscene, like talking about sex. Behind closed doors in our rooms with friends, we could giggle about intercourse—girls who *did it*, as we expressed it then; but unable to mention my father, I stifled my thoughts and suppressed my desire to confide in friends. I believed I held an enchanted secret that would betray Daddy if I asked or told anyone, so I suffered alone. Halting phrases, euphemisms, and diversions were meant to pacify us; they kept us silent and solitary with our thoughts and our sorrow, but they didn't remove the heartache. While children, we accepted the silence or the few comforting words and tried to forget that Daddy was "away." That was what was expected of us, and we were dutiful children. As I grew older, however, the knot that held my questions loosened, and I wanted some explanations.

II
*R*uth's *S*tory

6
George Abel Dreyfous

One afternoon after school, I walked the two blocks to St. Charles Avenue to catch the streetcar downtown. I don't recall what grade I was in or what year it was, but I must have been old enough to go shopping by myself on Canal Street. At twelve or thirteen, my friends and I frequently took the streetcar downtown after school to buy sweaters and skirts at Maison Blanche and lipstick and friendship bracelets at the dime store, but I planned to go alone on this quest. That noon, during lunch hour at school, I called my Uncle George at his office and told him I wanted to see him. I thought he might explain something about what happened to my father; a lawyer certainly would be able to give me facts. I told him I would take the streetcar to his office as soon as school was over. I didn't tell him why, and he didn't ask.

After looking down the tracks and seeing no streetcar in the distance, I sat crosslegged on the cement by the tracks, finished the cookie left over from lunch, and reviewed French verbs for tomorrow's test. As the streetcar rattled to a stop, I tucked my books under my arm, fished in my purse for the seven cents' fare, and sat down on one of the wood seats—in the front, of course, not behind the movable barrier separating whites from blacks. I finished writing the answer to the last question at the end of my history assignment as the streetcar screeched around Lee Circle, a few blocks from Unk's office.

As the car turned the circle, I looked up at the figure of General Robert E. Lee standing defiantly on the statue's tall pedestal and packed my pencil and eraser into my purse. A few moments later I rang the bell, and the car soon eased to a halt on Canal Street. I walked back down Carondelet to

Common Street and entered the busy commercial world of bankers and lawyers. The imposing Canal Bank Building that Unk worked in always awed me. I inevitably felt out of place there and fearful, but the dread might have been partly because I remembered summer earaches, riding this same elevator up to see the doctor on the fifth floor. When we had sore throats, he'd paint our throats with orange antiseptic, which made us gag when he forced the long swab down our throats. I was glad this trip downtown was to see Unk and not the ear, nose, and throat doctor. I'd chosen to talk to Unk, not only because of his legal knowledge: I had claimed him as a substitute father when Daddy went away, perhaps a fantasy that lingered.

When I pushed open the heavy door to the waiting room, I was greeted by the eyes of clients whose gaze followed me as I, dressed in pleated kilt, gray wool cardigan sweater buttoned backwards, Peter Pan dickie, saddle shoes and bobby socks, sailed through the crowded room, down the yellow hall, and past the opaque door of his partner's room to the closed door of my uncle's office. Before I could knock, the door swung in and an obese man, eyes covered with a gray hat, carrying a raincoat over his arm, brushed by me without a word. As I entered, my uncle stood up, greeted me, cleared ledgers and papers from the great leather-topped desk that had once belonged to Felix, and placed them in an open file drawer. In addition to the desk, which dominated the room, the office was furnished sparsely, with three ancient office chairs of yellow wood, several green metal cabinets, and a wood rack with a tarnished mirror and outstretched arms for coats and hats. No plants or curtains brightened the room; only his Harvard Law School diploma and other certificates decorated the walls. Venetian blinds hid the dusty windows. The austere order of the room, typical of offices of the time, informed clients of the serious purpose of their entering.

Unk greeted me with a polite kiss on the forehead and pointed to the chair in front of his desk. Wheeling his swivel chair around beside me, he sat down, crossed his bony legs, and clasped his fingers around his knees. I looked up at his gaunt face and saw a flicker of a smile move his thin lips slightly, as he waited for me to speak. We exchanged a few words about my schoolwork and then I stammered, "Unk . . . tell me. I want to know . . . I need to know what happened . . . to Daddy, I mean."

He didn't speak for minutes and then said in carefully chosen words and many pauses, "Well . . . your father made a mistake, you know . . . and . . .

er . . . he was involved with some people he trusted . . . and got mixed up with them." Unk stopped talking for a moment, uncrossed and recrossed his legs several times, adjusted the wire-rimmed glasses around his butterfly ears, and cleared his throat. He then launched into an incomprehensible explanation, interrupted frequently with throat clearings or an occasional "and" or an "um," and he used terms I did not understand in his attempt to enlighten me. Obviously embarrassed and unable—or unwilling—to simplify, he spoke haltingly and inarticulately about the case and the trial. Although I tried to listen, I could not follow what he was saying. I believed that somehow it was my fault that I could not understand. After he finished, I found no opening to probe into for further information. We talked briefly of other matters, and I left. On my way out of the building, I stopped at the newsstand and bought a Mars bar. As I chewed it on the way home, I tried to make sense of what he'd told me but soon gave up.

Although George researched meticulously and wrote with clarity, he struggled to express himself orally—even in less threatening situations. His speech seemed awkward, and his movements appeared clumsy. This shyness and unwieldiness never held him back from sports, political discourse, and activism but perhaps may have been the cause of his having remained a bachelor until the age of fifty-three, when he married Mathilde. Before this marriage in 1947, George lived on Audubon Place with his mother, father, and sister Ruth. He had known and perhaps loved Mathilde before she married, raised two sons, and was widowed, but George was painfully shy and undemonstrative. He showed his affection only with smiles. Although Unk was awkward and inarticulate—even with children—I was drawn to him and felt he cared about me. He taught me badminton: on Sundays after dinner, we played on the driveway court behind the house on Audubon Place. In his inarticulate manner, he encouraged me in many ways.

He also took me out on Lake Pontchartrain in his boat. I did not know then that George had bought the yacht in 1942 as a last desperate effort to join the war and fight the Nazis. He hated fascism so vehemently that he tried in 1939 to volunteer for the British armed forces. When they rejected him, he went to Canada to enlist. Not only did that fail, he was deported as well. In addition to trying to enlist in the British armed service, his hatred of fascism and Hitler led him to direct his efforts toward persuading the United States to support Great Britain with American armed forces. He wrote Hale Boggs, the newly elected Louisiana congressman, and wired Franklin D. Roosevelt, warning that "unless we can give more effective aid to the British Commonwealth we shall eventually face a struggle with Germany and Japan." Though unsuccessful in these efforts, his letter-writing campaign may have contributed to the congressional decision in 1941 to enact Lend Lease (the transfer of arms and equipment to Britain) shortly after his appeal.

When frustrated by negative responses to letters mailed to senators and officials, he wrote to the Red Cross and the president of B'nai B'rith to pressure them to organize field hospitals in France. In his yearning to get to the front, George thought he might face action, like Hemingway, in the driver's seat of an ambulance, but the B'nai B'rith spurned his idea for fear of being labeled warmongers by American anti-Semites. The Red Cross refused as well. The United States wasn't ready to join the war, even though George was.

With war declared, George, classified 4-F, bought the yacht and offered it to the Coast Guard: he had heard that cruisers were needed desperately. Not only did they gladly accept the boat, but in exchange for it they trained him, taught him navigation, and made him a lieutenant. Once in the Coast Guard, he and his seamen cruised the Caribbean, searching for enemy submarines for the remainder of the war.

George practiced law with his father in the firm founded in 1843 by his grandfather, Abel Dreyfous. George's zeal for justice and human rights, however, steered him to causes outside of his private law practice: for example, fighting for constitutional rights with the American Civil Liberties Union (ACLU) and struggling for civil rights, first with the Louisiana League for Constitutional Rights and then with the Urban League. Through letters, newspaper articles, and financial contributions, he supported victims of injustice in New Orleans, especially poor black people arrested unfairly in the city. I knew from scanning his bookshelves that George read avidly about politics, but I was unaware of his zealous involvement in contemporary events. Perhaps because he still considered me a child, even after I had a family of my own, he never spoke to me about his activities—our conversations never touched his passion for justice. I suppose he thought I wouldn't be interested; why, I do not know. Later, when I did learn about it, I was proud to hear about the outrage he voiced over segregation and his activism during the McCarthy era—speaking out as an advocate for individuals like Owen Lattimore, but it wasn't part of his nature to seek acclaim for doing what he thought was right.

George was engaged in defending civil liberties and the constitution long before the McCarthy era and even before World War II. In 1937, when four Tulane University professors were charged with subversion by a right-wing group, George was outraged. Although they were cleared of the charges, two of them later joined other professors in protesting university policies. Speaking out against the university offended the board of trustees and caused the relationship between the professors and the university to become so strained that these men—most of them not tenured—could no longer teach there and soon left for other places. Alarmed by this violation of academic freedom and by other situations affecting free expression, George and other men and women organized the Louisiana League for the Preservation of Constitutional Rights. The league became involved in many cases: from defending the owner of a bookstore arrested for selling "subversive" books, one of which was by Upton Sinclair, to more dangerous activities involving violence against union leaders. Even though some of these organizers were members of the Communist Party, the league intervened to protect the free speech of the union leaders and to support them in their mission—which was to help poor black farm laborers who were being exploited by white planters.

George went down to St. John the Baptist Parish as advocate for a Congress of Industrial Organizations (CIO) activist who had been arrested while attempting to unionize these farmworkers—most of whom were black. When he arrived there, George discovered that the site for the hearing was the judge's favorite tavern. Not himself a drinker and unaccustomed to frequenting bars, George adapted to the judge's method of negotiating, which consisted of taking turns buying rounds of drinks—a novel way of persuading a judge to reduce bail. Of course, by going there to protect a union organizer, who happened also to be a communist, George was labeled a "Communist Nigger-lover Jew" and risked being physically beaten or even shot, for these were not gentle times. Rebelling now against the beliefs and values of the South, this was the same George who, when a boy, hung a picture in his room of his hero, Robert E. Lee and, when he was a little older, spat at the statue of Abraham Lincoln.

Throughout the late thirties and early forties, the league was engaged in defending the constitutional rights of the vulnerable, and George—the prime mover of this organization, a man who feared violence and confrontation—spoke out and acted, placing himself once again in danger of being beaten, as many had been. He fought for the rights of Jehovah's Witnesses and defended victims of police brutality, most of whom were black. Here was a man who, a few years earlier, had fired the "colored" upstairs maid for forgetting to call him "Sir."

Although the letters and newspaper articles he wrote provoked angry responses to his radical, unpopular positions—even threats—the first time he found himself facing physical aggression by a shoving and screaming mob was when he opposed segregation laws before they were taken off the books in Louisiana. Basically an idealistic, peaceful, and timid man, George couldn't even stand the sight of blood on a cut finger. He was unaccustomed to fighting, but he risked his personal safety by supporting unpopular and volatile causes because he valued justice—and that was prior to his marriage to Mathilde Schwab. When they married and she moved to New Orleans, Mathilde joined hands with him in the fight for equality throughout the civil rights movement, for the rest of his life and for years after his death. Once the civil rights law mandated school integration, as a member of Save Our Schools (SOS), a citizens' group organized in 1959, George, with Mathilde's endorsement, fought against the powerful leaders who tried to close the schools rather than allow Negro children to attend with whites. When the city blocked funds to the school board for teachers' salaries, George and others loaned money to the board to pay teachers in the three schools targeted for integration. Then, in spite of his fearful nature, George found himself surrounded in the street by a dangerous mob when he and others tried to protect a lone Negro child as she attempted to cross the lines of protesters and enter the school. I never knew about his courageous stance until someone sent me an article about it long after the event. And now that years have passed and writers have finally chronicled the civil rights movement, including this shameful occurrence, the black child has become known by her given name, Ruby Bridges, because her story and those of other courageous African Americans can now be told without fear of reprisals.

As the newspapers reported, that clash occurred on a sunny and cold

December morning in 1960, when George and some other people braved the chill and drove to the Frantz School to escort six white students and a Negro girl to school. Forty angry white "housewives" ("cheerleaders," as the newspapers described them), who had blockaded the newly segregated school, cursed, spat upon, kicked, and hit the people who helped "sneak" children into the building. At first, the mob had rained blows and hurled stones at a white Tulane graduate student whom they recognized for having participated previously in a sit-in that resulted in his being arrested and charged with criminal anarchy. Once the police helped this man get away, the crowd—kicking, spitting, and screaming "Communists" and "nigger lovers"—chased George and the others until the police rescued them and guided them safely to their cars. Later, Mathilde's name was among those listed in a newspaper article as owning one of the cars used to "haul" the children into school. The Louisiana Association of Citizens Councils wanted these names given to the Committee on Un-American Activities of the Louisiana legislature. Southern bigots dumped all liberals into one Communist carton, and those with Jewish names were doubly despised.

While Unk was involved in all these events, I was living in Connecticut, totally immersed in childrearing. Then, less than three months after the school integration episode, my aunt called to tell me Unk was in the hospital with hepatitis, which some family members thought was caused by his eating raw oysters. Several days later, he died at the age of sixty-six. I never again had the opportunity to try to question him about Daddy. I wonder, would he ever have divulged his perception of the truth?

As Mother, Alby, and I sat on the terrace devouring crabs that sunny February in 1993, I thought about Unk and my journey to his office to find answers to my questions. I wondered if his inarticulate explanation was caused by embarrassment, an incapacity to communicate in plain speech, or an unwillingness to break a silence; then, I thought, perhaps I blocked out his explanation. In any case, I am unable to discover the motivation behind his inability or refusal to communicate. I looked at Mother and pondered whether Unk ever told her that I had gone that afternoon to his office. Knowing George and his code of ethics, I felt certain he had never informed her. Just as he honored the confidentiality of clients, I believe he kept our conference private.

I wonder whether she and her brother ever communicated about Leon's situation. Other than recommending a lawyer or what course of action to take, I doubt that George had talked much with Caroline about my father. The perplexing question remains unanswered: if George defended strangers against injustice, what was his stance during my father's trials? If my father suffered persecution by unfair legal practices and a loaded jury, as Mother claims, did George protest? Did he agree with Mother and numerous other people that Daddy was an innocent victim? If he believed that, why didn't Unk voice it to me? And how did his brother Julius emerge unscathed? Did Daddy take a fall for him, as several persons phrased it—with George not intervening? Mother's ambiguous answers skirt my questions. The silence, like a protective shell, remains unbroken.

A mockingbird's chatter awakened me from my reflections, and I saw that Mother looked tired. We piled the empty crab shells onto a tray and helped Rosie wheel Mother through the narrow French doors from the terrace to the solarium. After we lifted her from her wheelchair to her stair chair, we watched her bump her way upstairs, waving and smiling all the way up. Soon after she disappeared around the landing and we heard her being wheeled to her bedroom, Alby and I left in her maroon Oldsmobile for Ruth's house. When in New Orleans, I like to spend part of each day with her, listening to her stories.

We drove down oak-lined St. Charles Avenue, over whose wide neutral ground streetcars rattle on tracks running between camellia bushes, oleanders, and palm trees. Ruth told me that only in New Orleans is the area between two sides of a divided avenue called a "neutral ground," and she related several tales about the origin of that phrase. Some say it was coined during the Civil War, when the street was neutral territory separating northerners from southerners. Others claim it originated when Canal Street served as a safe zone between the Creoles in the Quarter and the Americans on the other side. Probably, Ruth surmised, when the canal was filled on Canal Street, it was called a neutral ground because no one owned that strip of land. I liked the more romantic explanations, even though they may be apocryphal. In any case, the neutral ground creates the illusion of wide streets, allowing us to enjoy the beauty of the homes and gardens on St. Charles Avenue. As we drove downtown, I realized what a Yankee I had become: I found I had to adjust once again to the crawling traffic as we passed by the stately houses—some of which replicate antebellum plantations and are surrounded by azaleas and magnolia trees. Some of the branches still blossomed with green and orange glass beads—remnants of Mardi Gras parades, when costumed people on gaudy floats throw them to the crowds below. These beads on the budding trees symbolize the dualities of this city—the romantic past sleeping just beneath a panoply of decadence: bigotry, corruption, demagoguery even, debauchery, and exploitation. Because of the sensuous beauty of the city, often I see moonlight on a stormy night—I forget to notice the ugliness and corruption beneath the polished surfaces.

Before reaching the Garden District, where Ruth lives, I suddenly spotted the Roman taffy man's horse-drawn wagon parked in front of a Baptist church. Fortunately, the slow-moving traffic along St. Charles allowed me to swerve to the curb and park behind his red-and-white cart. At his window, I bought several sticks of pink, white, and brown sticky taffy from the old man (the grandson of the original candy man), who drives the family wagon, a vestige from the old days, along Uptown streets.

That candy reminded me of when I used to sneak two blocks down Millaudon Street to buy penny candy from Sarge's Sweet Shop, a dingy, unpainted one-room shack, not much larger than an outhouse. I don't remember being told I couldn't go there, but I know we weren't allowed to wander far from our fenced-in play yard until we were old enough to play kick-the-can in the road in front of the house after dinner or take the streetcar alone to school in the morning. I suppose the reason that we felt we shouldn't go there was that Sarge's, unlike most places in the segregated South, was frequented by both white children and "colored," as we said back then. Despite the "separate but equal" public schools, restrooms, and lunch counters, there were few segregated neighborhoods then, but we never played with colored children—or even spoke to them. In fact, our entire neighborhood, from the Mississippi River to St. Charles Avenue and Broadway, is a historic district called "the Black Pearl" since so many black families reside around us, some of whom have lived there for many generations. Eula, my mother's former cook, still lives there in a shotgun cottage crowded with antiques that she has bought at estate sales over the years. Now when she needs to pay for unexpected repairs to her house, she sells a piece or two. I love to visit her when I'm in New Orleans and hear her tell me from which white family she bought her treasures. She's a rich source of stories about her family and mine. Her family came to New Orleans from the country—New Roads, where her father was a sharecropper. Eula's husband, Walter, came to work for us, too, before he got a job in the shipyards during the war. We celebrated her eightieth birthday over dinner on one of our trips home to New Orleans.

Sarge catered to everyone. When my friend Peggy and I used to get off the streetcar after school, we would knock at the back door of the old unpainted stone and wood mansion on St. Charles and Lowerline and beg for free samples of potato chips from an old woman who manufactured them in her basement. Then, before going home, we would walk down Broadway, cutting across a side street, skirting our houses so we could sneak to Sarge's store. From the glass bins on the counter we'd select Tootsie Rolls, licorice strings, or pink bubble gum wrapped in two pieces of paper—one a comic strip. We'd buy round licorice candies called "nigger babies." Sometimes in hot weather we'd spend our nickels on snowballs, scoops of shaved ice served in paper cups and covered with sticky strawberry, cherry, or chocolate syrup.

Max Tropez, who sometimes drives my mother to her doctor's appointments, told me last spring that as a young boy he worked for Sarge, sweeping the floor of the sweet shop and selling newspapers. He used to jump on moving streetcars, run through selling papers, hop off one car and leap onto another, keeping a penny for each paper he sold at three cents a copy—dangerous work for a boy and for so little money. Child-labor laws didn't apply to Negro children during segregation. Aunt Ruth lobbied against this exploitation of children, but that came later, probably not until the late forties or fifties.

Max told me his parents had moved to our neighborhood in the city from Bayou Lafourche, near Donaldsonville, Louisiana, where his great-grandfather raised sugarcane on land granted to him as a free man after the Civil War. According to Max, his Hispanic grandfather, who married an Indian woman from a reservation, did little but sit on his porch all day, and the land was sold. That's when they came to New Orleans. Max drove supply trucks during World War II, seeing action in Italy, France, and Germany. His unit crossed over the Mediterranean from northern Africa when the Allies invaded Italy. Now that Max has retired from truck driving and lives close by on Oak Street, he chauffeurs elderly ladies to appointments and drives his grandchildren to school. One daughter is a nurse and the other is chief of pediatrics at a medical school in New Orleans, and some of the grandchildren attend Newman School. He told me he remembered my brother Bubby coming into Sarge's sweet shop to buy candy—that was when Max swept the floor there. I never knew him as my neighbor.

7
Ruth Dreyfous

Licking the sweet taffy, we rang the bell at Ruth's garden gate, which buzzed its death rattle back at us, releasing the lock. Alby and I entered her shady garden, which is protected from the street by a brick wall on one side and great bushes and chain-link fences on the other sides. Once inside the gate, we felt the looming presence of the live oak tree at the center of her garden. It was cool under the enormous limbs that shade the grassy patch of her yard: one limb of the tree arches over and touches her bedroom roof; another bends itself over the roof of the house on the other side of the garden. Ruth's ranch and that other house, which used to belong to George and Mathilde, were built after Ruth sold the Audubon Place family home in 1955. Their brother Julius designed the two 1950s modern houses between twin oak trees, named the Newcomb Oaks after the college, Tulane's sister school, which formerly had its campus on this land in the Garden District.

We walked up the path past flower beds crowded with giant tropical plants, a sprinkling of daffodils, and a bird-of-paradise just beginning to blossom. When he lived there and they shared the garden, Unk preferred variegated green plants to riots of color in a garden; he felt flowers weren't restful, and they distracted him from his thoughts. Wanting order within his house as well, he and Mathilde chose modern furnishings for their rooms. That was after Ruth had auctioned off most of the Victorian artifacts from the Audubon Place house: Oriental rugs, French vases, brocaded chairs, and antique tables that over the years her parents had collected for their home.

When my grandparents, Felix and Julia, planned to move from their white-frame, neoclassic house on Jackson Avenue, Julius designed the Italianate house on Audubon Place for them. Many of their Jewish friends were moving farther uptown, and the new stucco house, with carved moldings, wide halls, and grand staircase, symbolized their further assimilation into fashionable New Orleans society, miles away from the Creole neighborhood in the French Quarter where they began their married life and far from their home on Jackson Avenue.

Even when they lived midtown, in the large Jackson Avenue house, Felix and Julia were assimilated into New Orleans society. Their names and "reception day" appeared in the social register along with a few others from prominent Jewish families with wealth, position, and longevity in the city. Names like Kohlmeyer, Feibleman, Godchaux, and Cahn were listed on the same pages as Favrot, Beauregard, Dufour, and Dunbar. Having a reception day meant that on the designated Wednesday afternoon, a lady was expected to be at home to receive callers. If for some reason Julia was indisposed on a Wednesday, women left their engraved calling cards on a silver tray in the front hall. According to the *New Orleans Social Register* of 1904, Mr. and Mrs. Felix Dreyfous and Mr. and Mrs. Abel Dreyfous would be at home at 1140 Jackson Avenue every Wednesday, and their cousin, Jules Dreyfous, would be at his home at 2840 St. Charles Avenue on Thursday. Since Abel had died in 1892, I wonder why his name still appeared in the 1904 social register.

Although Felix and Julia rarely attended services, because Felix didn't like sermons and thought the rabbi mumbled his words, they maintained their affiliation with the Jewish temple downtown and observed some of the holidays, particularly Passover, by celebrating with a family *seder*. But their social life did not revolve around Temple Sinai. Since Julia belonged to the Orléans Club, an exclusive (primarily Gentile) women's society housed in one of the elegant mansions on St. Charles Avenue, she dined there for luncheons several days a week and spent afternoons discussing current events with a group of women friends. Felix occupied his busy days practicing law, serving on boards of institutions, and contributing time to cultural and civic affairs.

Even though they were not big socializers, some weekends Felix played cards with other gentlemen and in the evening attended balls or other events with Julia at the Harmony Club, a prestigious Jewish club organized as a substitute for the elite Gentile Boston and Pickwick clubs, from which even the Jewish aristocracy was excluded. Rich businessmen, those who controlled the social and economic power of the city, saw these clubs as private havens—the last bastion of Christian unity. Although Jewish men were never asked to participate in meetings or lunch at these clubs, some Jewish families were invited to balls in the early years of Mardi Gras—before the carnival season evolved into the ultimate extravaganza of wealth and power. Once that happened, the fantasy of royalty was played out with such pretense that the kings and queens of Mardi Gras began to exercise their imperial power. As Mardi Gras gradually developed into a competitive world run by an exclusive Gentile oligarchy, the climate changed toward Jews.

Except for these carnival activities, which they pretended to ignore, Julia and Felix felt accepted in Uptown New Orleans society, as did most of their friends. Others were annoyed at being excluded, and a few families arranged trips abroad in order to be out of town during "the season." Julia told my mother that Jews were excluded from balls because one year a Jewish man had brought a woman from a fancy brothel as his guest. Whether Julia's explanation was a fabrication, an exaggeration, or was based on an actuality (some man's inappropriate acting out of his fantasy, which then was blamed on the Jews), Julia probably believed in it to assuage her wounded feelings at not being included. She and her Jewish friends tried to hide their feelings and make believe nothing had changed. One of Julia's friends, Bertie Finegold, enjoyed going to her Christian friends' houses and, like a modern-day Cinderella, watch them all dressing up in their carnival ball gowns and preparing themselves for an event to which she was not welcome. She stopped going to their houses to admire them this way when her daughter Rose explained why it was wrong to do that.

While Jews experienced more exclusion from dinners and parties as carnival became more and more the center of the social season in the 1880s and as economic changes in the country occurred, Felix never felt that the new tide of anti-Semitism affected his legal practice or his cultural and civic activities. The same wealthy businessmen who spurned him in the evening eagerly sought his advice during the day, as clients in his office and as colleagues on boards and committees.

Some of the Jewish members of the community attributed the change in attitude of the Gentiles to the arrival in the city of a few Russian Jews, with their conspicuous ethnic dress and behavior. Before this time, a few Orthodox Jews lived downtown on Dryades Street near their synagogue, but the butcher in the market was the only contact Uptown Jews had with any of them. This new group of immigrants not only was a source of embarrassment to the assimilated Jews but also was a problem for Jewish agencies which, although sympathetic, were concerned about the economic burden of giving financial help to these new families. Giving them charity when so many others in the community needed assistance stirred up controversy. Some felt that even though these new people had fled from pogroms in Russia or Poland and arrived in New Orleans as refugees without money or jobs, supporting them was not the responsibility of the Jewish charities. One rabbi even took the position that only poor people with the potential for being contributing members of the community should be helped and that these newcomers would always be a burden. In contrast, Rabbi Max Heller of Temple Sinai, motivated by a belief that all needy people deserved assistance and despite criticism from his own congregation, tried to persuade the city's Jewish leaders to come to the aid of these unfortunate people.

One way of providing for new Russian immigrants was to assist them in resettling, like homesteaders, on rural land. Arrangements were made for one such group to come to New Orleans, leave their wives behind in the city temporarily, and begin an agricultural community in Catahoula Parish, miles north of the city. The charter for this Sicily Island project, the First Agricultural Colony of Israelites in America, was drafted and signed in 1881, with Felix as notary and his father, Abel, as witness. About thirty-five men "temporarily of this city" signed the agreement and went off to settle the new territory. The experiment failed when floods destroyed the crops, the men became lonely, and many of them contracted malaria. A few months later, they abandoned the farm. Some of the newcomers found other ways to make a living in the city; most went elsewhere, roaming the South as peddlers.

Since both Julia and Felix came from prominent families of wealth and position, they were assimilated into the greater community from the time they married. Despite their exclusion from certain Mardi Gras events and from the downtown clubs, they believed they were acceptable in the eyes of their Christian neighbors. For this reason, Felix and most of the other members of Temple Sinai were staunch anti-Zionists. This caused fierce arguments with Rabbi Heller, who was one of the only Reformed clergymen in the country to preach Zionism. Early on, Felix and George opposed him, believing themselves to be Americans and not citizens of a Jewish nation.

As Felix expressed it in one of his letters to George in 1914, "There are certainly some good reasons on the part of Jews to favor the restoration of the Kingdom of Judea but it has not as yet been satisfactorily explained to me why people following a certain faith should want temporal power." Felix's letter argues that Jews of different nationalities could not live in unity, because "their language, habits and thoughts will . . . clash and discord will be ever constant . . . [and] . . . how could the Zionist prevent a preponderance, in the course of time, of Christians and Mohammetans which would bring about the overthrow of the Jewish factions?"

The move to their elaborate new house on Audubon Place felt natural to Felix and Julia and was further evidence of their place in society. Julius' taste for the ornate, as evidenced in this house—the antithesis of my father's less pretentious designs—suited them perfectly during the era in which they lived there. Yet in the fifties the house and the furnishings seemed inappropriate to Ruth and George. When they moved back to the gentrified Garden District, both new houses reflected a desire for simplicity. Inside their homes, wall-to-wall carpeting and modern Danish tables and chairs replaced Oriental rugs and antique furnishings, and most of the walls were covered with grass cloth in the style of the fifties. The opulence associated with pride of possessions and desire for social acceptance, which seemed correct to my grandparents in the twenties, no longer felt appropriate to my aunt and uncle. Social awareness and a heightened consciousness in the fifties motivated my aunt and uncle to divest themselves of their parents' treasures; they traded belongings for unencumbered living and more time to participate in the community.

When we arrived at Ruth's front door, she was standing there bent over a walker, wearing wraparound dark green glasses, which protected her cataract eyes from the sudden blast of sunlight that greeted her when she opened the door. Her gray hair fell unevenly, flattened on one side from her just having arisen from bed; but even though her frail body was failing her, her smile emanated from a kernel of spirit still flowering inside. When she uttered her hello, her childlike voice reminded me of similar welcomes when, as a child, we visited "Ru-tee," as we called her then. Even now, whenever she sees children, especially babies, she calls herself that name and cries out, "*Ach . . . ach der liebe!*" or "Angel!" Never having had a child of her own, she doted on everyone else's babies and collected miniature angels from all over the world, keeping them on glass shelves, like Laura's menagerie in Tennessee Williams' play.

As I looked at her, I recalled the times we traveled together, when I had to exert myself to keep up with her pace, for she had been an avid sightseer and enjoyed showing other people her favorite places. Not too many years ago, Alby and I took our children to Europe for a summer vacation. We wanted to introduce them to cathedrals, castles, and museums, and we planned to wander through river valleys and plains. Our meandering pace changed dramatically when we met Ruth, who led us through city and countryside, not only wanting us to learn from her vast knowledge but also wishing to share her enthusiasm for what she loved best in Europe.

Despite the accelerated tempo, our children preferred Ruth's one-hour museum tours to my thorough three-hour ones. They hated my compulsive need to visit every object in a museum, and they loved the way Ruth moved through the building, giving them a crash course in culture. She decided what works of art they should see, knew where to find each one, and told them what details to observe. Her ability to communicate with young children, to capture and hold their attention, reflects her devotion to children and her innate ability to teach. From experience gained by reading and traveling, she developed a passion for music, art, and literature, which she believes children ought to learn about at an early age. Our children listened to her as if her words were the Ten Commandments that they were required to learn by heart.

Even with her knowledge and skill, as a child I never felt easy when she came into my classroom at school—especially when I was in high school. I suppose that might have been embarrassment before my peers—having my aunt, the school psychologist, come to administer standardized tests to my class, but she came into the room brimming with confidence, and the children responded to her directions. I kept my eyes on my desk, hoping mine would not meet hers.

Our children are adults now, but they still talk about the paintings she made them see and how she knew without consulting museum guides where each was located. Our family recalls that before entering the Rijksmuseum in Amsterdam, she said, "Now, when we go in, we'll just go right to the middle room in the left wing on the second floor. You have to look at the painting on the back wall. It's *The Night Watch*, the most important Rembrandt in the whole world . . . then we'll see Vermeer's *Young Woman in Blue Reading a Letter* in the next room." Although the museum is a labyrinth of rooms and corridors and she had not been there in several years, we found the paintings right where she told us they would be.

Like a sudden summer storm, we swept through Denmark that summer with her, visiting in one day what most tourists see in three, for she knew what our children would like and what they should see: in addition to Tivoli Gardens and stores like Den Permanante, we explored Hamlet's Elsinore, Hans Christian Andersen's village, a Viking museum, and the countryside outside of Copenhagen. But unlike the typical tour guide barking facts at tourists, she stood back and let us absorb our impressions.

Ruth's memory for details and events even now astonishes me. I believe that her sharpness, assertiveness, and sense of direction led her to accumulate facts on her travels not only for her pleasure or for dinner-party conversation; she also used her observations and channeled her energy to work for social change. Her knowledge of history and her appreciation for her position in the community inspired Ruth to become an activist like her father and George; she led others in the fight for programs for people— especially children. Having none of her own, she became an advocate for all children, diverting her devotion to young people and sparking her natural energy into action. Like her father before her, Ruth believed her affluence did not entitle her to live a life of easy comfort, indifferent to the needs of disadvantaged people around her.

I first journeyed with Ruth the summer of 1940, when I was eight. She took me on my first long train ride, to New York and on to New England, where we drove through the Berkshires, to Boston, and then up to Maine. We had picked up Ruth's car at Pennsylvania Station; since an automobile could be shipped by rail to one's destination in those days, we didn't need to rent a car for our tour of New England. I learned map reading and gained a sense of time and space as I sat next to her on the long drive.

One night, we checked into a weather-beaten old inn on the Maine coast. All night long, the wind howled and rain beat against the panes of our room. Next morning when we awoke, I saw the flattened dune grass and at breakfast discovered that we had slept through a fierce storm. At that time no radar warned of hurricanes, and we had spent the night with a dangerous one. While in Maine, we looked at summer camps for my sister, stayed overnight at a family camp, and hiked around the White Mountains. For a child who had never seen a mountain except for a fake hill built in Audubon Park by the WPA to show children what one looked like, New England's mountainous landscape seemed like a dream tapestry.

After leaving New Hampshire, we drove back to New York and shipped the car home to New Orleans. During our New York stay, we ate every night at the Automat because I thought it was the best restaurant I had ever eaten at, and Ruth enjoyed watching me put nickels in those magic windows that opened and served up sandwiches or lemon-meringue pie. Even though she probably would have chosen more elegant eating places had I not been with her, she let me select the restaurant.

When my mother agreed to let me go, she made Ruth promise not to leave me alone at night with strangers, to keep me with her day and night. To comply, I went with her on her date with Joe Levy, a former beau, who took us several nights to the New York World's Fair. When we were in Massachusetts, late one night under the stars at Tanglewood I heard the Boston Symphony Orchestra perform. Whenever I go there now, I remember when I first saw those tall pine trees, dark against the dusky sky, and heard the woodwinds, strings, and choir fill the music shed with Bach's B-minor mass.

When I returned from that trip with Ruth, I told my mother that I was not ever going to get married. I wanted to live like Ruth and travel the rest of my life. From my eight-year-old perspective, journeying from place to place, being bombarded with images and new experiences, seemed the best way to live; I did not understand that travel could not quiet desire. I could see nothing missing in Ruth's life, for I did not know the loneliness that plagued her from having no children of her own. Also, what I did not know was this journey's purpose—to protect me and to find a summer retreat for my sister—to keep us innocent and untouched and out of way of the pain and anxiety howling about Mother and Daddy, for that was the summer of my father's trials.

Ruth took me away to escape that fierce and dangerous storm in Louisiana. She never hinted about what was occurring there with my parents, never talked to me about them while we were together that summer, and I never questioned why she took me away on that journey. It was only just recently that I connected the year of my parents' nightmare to this special excursion with Ruth.

Before that trip, Ruth had spent most summers traveling to Europe, stopping in all her familiar places and attending theater, opera, and concerts in Vienna, London, or Salzburg. In 1938, however, on a visit to France, Switzerland, and England, she recognized the signs of war. Feeling a strong sense of impending disaster, soon after she returned she wrote a memoir entitled "Eyewitness View of the Prologue to the Second World War," in which she detailed her impressions and recorded events she had seen and heard that summer. Having been a history major at Newcomb College, she felt compelled to record what she knew was history in the making.

Her narrative interpreted France's "gigantic preparations" to receive the king of England as France's attempt to show loyalty to Britain. She described French and Italian troop maneuvers on both sides of Mont Blanc in Chamonix, commenting, "How ridiculous it seemed to think of Mt. Blanc as a fortress." She observed more obvious signs in Switzerland— actualities of war, such as fortifications, cannons, soldiers, and fleeing refugees—she also had heard frightening accounts of Hitler's barbaric treatment of Jews. Although England seemed peaceful when she first arrived, Ruth perceived the readiness for war by the end of her visit there: she described the tension she felt at an outdoor performance of Shakespeare, when the buzzing of airplanes flying overhead conflicted with the poetry of *A Midsummer Night's Dream*. Before leaving England in September, she wrote that the country had begun war preparations by digging trenches in the parks, constructing shelters in subways, and outfitting people with gas masks. That trip to Europe was her last until the end of the war.

Now that her travel days are over, she stays home with clippings and letters, reflecting on memories she collected on her journeys and listening to recordings of great music she once heard live. There is perhaps no moment or event in her long life that does not have a permanent place in her recollections. With a historian's accuracy, she has chronicled significant events she witnessed during her ninety-three years, just as she has recorded exactly where in major museums her favorite paintings hang.

That afternoon, after ushering Alby and me into her living room, she offered us iced coffee, and the three of us settled down on the lumpy cushions of her Danish modern sofa and love seat, the L-shaped arrangement that dominates the large room. Although unable to see them now, on the long coffee table in front of us Ruth had stacked old programs from Salzburg music festivals, treasured letters, and framed photographs of the latest grandnieces and grandnephews—her new angels. It seemed like dusk inside, even though one whole side of her living room has floor-to-ceiling sliding-glass doors, for the Thai silk curtains filtered out the afternoon sunlight and screened the view of the oak tree in her shady garden.

"If I had married," she told me that afternoon, "I wouldn't have accomplished as much. It was a sacrifice. . . . Oh, I had chances, but I was not infatuated with anyone in particular. I was not coquettish . . . but I always had children that were devoted." She stopped, took a sip of iced coffee to check the dry cough that plagued her. "When I began going with boys and we used to have parties, I wasn't very good at socializing—kissing and all that foolishness. No, I was tall for a southern girl . . . and most of the boys were short. . . . Also, I was too good at sports. George always thought he was good, but I was better. . . . I shouldn't have beat so many boys." For a moment, I thought I heard regret in her voice for not having married, but then she went on to say that not having had children was her only sorrow in choosing a single life.

I looked across the room at the massive mahogany roll-top desk that had belonged to her father, which, she told me, he used to work at by the light of a green-shaded lamp evenings in the house on Audubon Place. The desk—the only piece of furniture she brought to her new house—now sits like a religious relic in an alcove especially designed for it, lit from above by recessed spotlights. Today, letters and photographs fill the drawers that once held her father's legal briefs, abstracts, and leases, for Ruth is the self-appointed custodian of his legacy and has spent the past few years sorting through his papers. Although she's nearly blind, she knows where to find everything in that house, whatever paper or book she wants. "Go over to the desk, Leta. I want you to bring me Father's history that he wrote. . . . No, no, it's on the left-hand side right there." No one dares move a thing.

As we sipped iced coffee and visited, I heard the chopping of a knife on a wood block in the kitchen and the soft humming of hymns as Alma prepared crawfish étouffé for our dinner with Ruth that night. The pungent smell of onions cooking for the roux and Alma's voice drifted through the open door into the living room. On the sofa next to me lay a pile of papers that Ruth had asked me to bring to her. When I looked for them in the den, they had been on one of the Danish sofabeds with some other books and papers, separate from the neat boxes stacked along one wall. Those are her father's papers, which she has been cataloging and placing in carefully labeled archival boxes, with the help of a Tulane student who comes to read to her.

I am familiar with the piles she requested, for they are the ones she keeps next to her chair in that room; she wants me to look at them each time I come. The documents in them reveal the story of Ruth's social activism, for, like George, she worked for school integration, equal educational opportunity, and poverty programs as the South struggled for civil rights. "Here, look at this," she commanded as she felt the cover of the document she held out to me, trying to see it with her fingers. "It's a resolution from the city council." I looked at the formal certificate of merit and put it aside as she handed me a leather folder that looked like an ordinary college diploma. "That's the Whitney Young Award for civil rights. The Urban League gave it to me at a dinner last year they had for me." She pulled from the pile on her lap the ACLU Ben Smith Award and held it close to her face. "I can't see it. . . . Read it." I read the words of commendation for her pioneering civil rights work. "Yes," she murmured, "I followed in Father's footsteps. He was the one who fought all his life to help people. Father always told me to do whatever I wanted to do . . . not to worry about making a living, but to do something to help others.

"I guess it began when I was in high school and volunteered at Kingsley House in the Irish Channel. That was the first settlement house in the city," she explained. "I used to play with the children, teach them ball, or take them on trips. Our chauffeur used to drive us. . . . Then in 1938, after I got my master's in child guidance from Columbia, I wanted the public schools to let me set up a remedial reading program, but the superintendent thought that would be a 'frill' they couldn't afford. The next year, though, I did help set up a testing program—evaluating students and making recommendations. Before that time, no achievement tests were given here.

"But I guess I really became involved as an activist during the Johnson era, when I went to work for Total Community Action. We organized people to get rid of junk in the streets—old cars and trash. Then I set up a program at Laurel and Jackson schools—a special crisis class for children repeatedly suspended or expelled . . . with the best teachers. I knew those children belonged in school and not out on the streets. That's why Mayor Moon Landrieu gave me the key to the city, and the Urban League honored me."

I looked at the stack of papers that tells the story of a woman who traveled alone, finding her way up some daring roads, and they represent her contribution to the city. Instead of offspring to call her own, these documents remind her of the meaning of her life.

She glanced down at the pile next to me on the sofa and sat silently rubbing her hands together. After a wordless moment, she looked up at a tall silver bowl, the *Times-Picayune* Loving Cup, that sits on a nearby table, and continued. "But it was the example of my father. . . . He was the one who started the Milne Boys Home for delinquents. Before that, the boys were sent to a terrible prison. He became president of the home. Because of all his work for these children, the newspaper presented him with that bowl. . . . I explain my life by the example of my father." As I listened to her, I glanced away from her pensive face and trembling fingers and looked at the desk in its alcove. I thought, we two women have this in common: while I have been searching for my father, Ruth has been memorializing hers. I settled back to listen.

8

Felix Jonathan Dreyfous

*O*nce again Ruth repeated the story she's so fond of narrating, about how her father was expelled from school as a young child. "It happened during Reconstruction, when the city was occupied. These were terrible times for the South. People were still smarting from the war, from times like when Silver Spoon Butler went house to house collecting spoons—taking people's silver. I don't know if that story is true, but that's what I was told. . . . oh, he was feared and despised. . . . And then during the occupation there were shortages of food and clothing in the city. The Union armies took everything for themselves and wanted patriotism to the North. . . . They made a rule that the schoolchildren had to stand and sing 'The Star-Spangled Banner.' Father refused. . . . He was a rebel, you know . . . and was expelled from public school. That's when they sent him to a private French school."

With eight other children in the family, I wonder how his parents responded to Felix's defiance. Times were hard for the city during Reconstruction, and Abel struggled through the years to support his large family; but Felix grew to be the one to follow in his father's path and widen it toward vaster fields. Once he finished school, Felix entered his father's firm, first as an errand boy in 1871 and then as a notary in 1876. After completing evening courses, he received his notarial commission in 1881 and his law diploma in 1888. He left his father's practice that same year, when he ran on the anti-lottery ticket and was elected state representative—to serve in the first reform legislature in Louisiana since Reconstruction.

During his term of office in Baton Rouge, he voted against the Louisiana lottery, which had been in existence since Reconstruction; he saw the corrupt way it was administered and thought that it taxed the poor for the benefit of the wealthy. Although many prominent New Orleans businessmen favored the lottery, Felix and other reformers successfully garnered enough votes to defeat it. That same year, Felix introduced a bill that created a police board to regulate the protection of the city of New Orleans—a reform that was profoundly needed to disengage police work from politics and rid the city of corruption.

A letter to Julia in 1897 reveals both his dismay over the lawlessness in the city and his optimistic spirit: "Really there are times when I feel as though it were folly to offer to reform the elements that constitute our population.—I nevertheless derived some comfort in the hope that the day will come when patriotism and the love of truth will triumph."

Having a broad agenda, he also favored gun control laws. Other bills he helped pass led to reformed real estate practices that would protect both property owners and the state in land transactions.

Felix made an attempt to oppose Jim Crow—the laws that separated the races for the next six decades until they were declared unconstitutional in the 1950s. He voted against one House version of the segregation statute but ended up siding with the overwhelming majority on the final bill. When he sat on the city council in 1896, he objected to the passage of Jim Crow laws in New Orleans. It seems appropriate that more than sixty years later, imbued with his reformer principles, George and Ruth helped fight against the inequality of opportunity that had been established by law in Louisiana during their father's time in office.

During the 1890s session of the state legislature, Felix introduced floodcontrol legislation to keep the river from inundating the city—a chronic headache for New Orleans. The passage of these laws enabled the state and the city to find ways to prevent the Mississippi from overflowing its banks. As part of the act, the legislature created state levee boards; these organizations were given the authority to construct additional levees along the river. Felix became the first president of the Orleans Parish Levee Board. Since flooding from heavy rains still remained a problem, when Felix served on the city council a few years later, he helped draft legislation to solve the sewage and drainage problems of New Orleans. Under his leadership, the city constructed an exceptional system of drains with pumps that still empty most of the streets, except during extremely heavy downpours.

In reflecting on Felix's reform ideals, I can understand why Ruth feels her father's work inspired her. The sense of fairness and the belief in justice, which Felix began in 1888, passed from him to Unk and Ruth, establishing a tradition of activism and civic responsibility and a continuity from his generation to theirs. Felix's wisdom and fortitude kindled Ruth and George's fight against injustice.

Once Felix ended his term with the state legislature, he returned to New Orleans to resume his law practice with his father and to channel his energies toward city projects. He did manage to find time during this period to woo Julia Seeman, a young woman originally from Cincinnati now living in New Orleans. Her father, George Seeman, had been sent down to manage the New Orleans branch of the Lehman Brothers cotton brokerage firm.

Julia and Felix were married in 1891 at Temple Sinai, with Rabbi Heller officiating. "You know," Ruth reminded me, "Mother wore the Belgian rose point lace that your mother, Betty, you, and your daughter Cathy all wore at your respective weddings. It covered her head and flowed in a long train all the way to the floor. It was gorgeous." I keep that lace wedding train in blue tissue paper for the next generation of women in the family to treasure.

Ruth's boxes contain evidence of her father's achievements: yellowing newspaper clippings praising his efforts to improve conditions and enrich the city and state. His service to City Park and the art museum there were among his proudest accomplishments. Whenever visitors came to town, while Ruth was still able to drive, she took them first to the historic sights of the city: Royal Street, St. Louis Cathedral, the Cabildo, and the Mint, for example. She reserved her "fifty-dollar tour" for those who expressed enthusiasm for the city, but she never failed to drive to City Park and point out Dreyfous Avenue, the road named in tribute to her father for his efforts on behalf of the park and its art museum.

A year ago, Betty and I came down for the naming of an oak tree in City Park for Felix, as yet another acknowledgment of our grandfather's philanthropy. Like other oak trees in the park that have been named for city benefactors, one of the trees was singled out to be the Dreyfous Oak, as a memorial to him. Somehow, without her sight, Ruth led us that day to the tree that was to be named for him. We took some pictures of ourselves sitting on a branch that spread down to the ground, but no formal speech or reception seemed to have been planned at that time. We took Ruth home and celebrated with a big bowl of Alma's gumbo.

I looked up at the desk resting in the alcove between the bookshelves and tried to imagine my grandfather sitting there perusing ledgers or proposed House bills when he came home from Baton Rouge at the end of a long session in the capital. Ruth told me he always said that his mother Caroline's charity work, especially at the Ladies' Aid and Sewing Society, helped him get elected, because she was known by so many people. I wished I could remember more about Grandfather, but all I recall is an image of a quiet man, formal and yet kind to children. What I remember of my grandmother is an image of her sitting in front of her dressing table in her bedroom, brushing her long white hair or buffing her fingernails. Strangely, the women in Ruth's life—her mother, Julia, and her grandmother, Caroline— remain enigmatic to me, for Ruth reveals little about them. It seems that both excelled in their sphere of domesticity; for women of that time, no more was expected.

Ruth reached for the glass of iced coffee Alma had placed on the table beside her, took a sip, and continued. "Father expected all of his children to follow in his footsteps; but in looking back, it seems to me that I was the one who was most loyal to the city and, like him, devoted my life to the improvement of education, to children, and to different liberal groups— especially during the civil rights era.

"It's queer, George got his picture in the paper for helping to integrate the schools . . . when that angry mob attacked him . . . but we tried to avoid publicity when we went down to Plaquemines Parish to save the school. It could have been a dangerous thing to do, but when we were asked, we went . . . Mathilde and I. It was after George died, and we convinced some others to go over to Plaquemines Parish to teach the children. . . . We drove together in my car."

I drank the rest of my iced coffee and stared across the living room, trying to see the shadows of the oak tree through the crack between the drapes and to imagine these women driving away from their safe homes to cross the river into hostile territory. I wondered if they equivocated, or if anyone tried to dissuade them. Would her father have approved of her action? What gave them the courage to go? I turned my gaze back to Ruth's face growing more and more animated as she narrated her tale.

9
Saving Our Schools

There is no mark on the wall to measure the precise height of women.

—Virginia Woolf

*I*t was pouring as the five women piled into Ruth's Oldsmobile and headed out of the city, but rain wasn't the element they had to fight that day. Rain seemed a mere inconvenience, even though some of the city streets were already being inundated. Exactly what they were up against they did not know as they turned off Magazine Street and drove up the ramp onto the bridge high over the Mississippi River. During the 1960s anything could happen, and Judge John Minor Wisdom had just mandated integration for all the public schools in Louisiana. People were angry and afraid. Schools were closing as many white parents—those who could afford to—sent their children to just-opened private academies. Others kept their children at home. Anger, confusion, and fear reigned.

One evening soon after the mandate, Ruth was finishing dinner when the telephone rang. Her housekeeper answered and called her to the phone, saying that Judge Wisdom wished to speak to her right away. She placed her napkin on the table and went to answer it. "Yes, we'll go tomorrow," was her immediate response. Judge Wisdom had been told that Leander Perez, the "czar" of Plaquemines Parish, in defiance of federal law had threatened to close all the Plaquemines Parish schools in a move to defeat integration. Ruth knew that Leander Perez controlled politics and economics in his mineral-rich parish, deriving power as judge and as head of the levee board. Judge Wisdom informed Ruth that Perez had ordered the teachers to stay away from their classrooms; the judge also told her that Perez swore he would shoot any "Nigra" who tried to enter schools in his parish and vowed to preserve the parish from infiltrators. By challenging Perez, Ruth would be attempting to defeat someone who was an outspoken racist, a blatant anti-Semite, and a powerful advocate of segregation. She knew that his primary motivation was to protect his political power and private fortune, some of which was reportedly gained illegally, and that he was not interested in the schools or the children.

Ruth had heard Perez on the evening news and recognized that not only was tomorrow a historic moment, a turning point in the evolution of the entire civil rights movement, but that it probably was also a potentially explosive one. Speaking for the Justice Department, Judge Wisdom asked Ruth and other volunteers to go to Plaquemines Parish and teach, to defy Perez' fight against integration by keeping the school open. Without hesitating, Ruth said, "Mathilde and I will call the other league members and make arrangements."

She put down the phone and walked across the garden to her brother's house. It had started to drizzle a bit, and the leaves of the oak tree shuddered in the wind. The trunk, black from the rain, seemed ominous that night as Ruth passed by it and tapped on the sliding-glass door. Once inside and her mission explained, she and Mathilde took turns calling some of their friends on the board of the League of Women Voters, those who had already pledged their support of integration and had expressed their willingness to act. When they heard about this particular mission, only three women— Blondie, Helen, and Renna—agreed to go with Ruth and Mathilde. The others were too afraid.

Ruth didn't sleep much that night, for she had to start out before six the next morning to meet the other women and find the school in Belle Chasse before opening time. The women needed to be there to greet the children, for the regular teachers had walked out at the end of the school day the previous afternoon. Ruth wondered how the children would respond and if, as replacement teachers, they would be treated like scabs and threatened in some way. Who knew what crazy act some white Klansman might concoct? They also tried to forget that it was Friday the thirteenth.

Ruth worried that someone might burn a cross on her front lawn, and Blondie suggested calling someone they knew at the paper to ask that their names be kept out of the news. They tried to make light conversation to keep from thinking of the possible dangers as they crossed the bridge to drive into Plaquemines Parish. Although Ruth's ardent beliefs led her toward this unknown danger, her fear of public wrath disturbed her. She did not want to expose the Dreyfous name. She wondered if her father would want her to take this risk. Ruth looked down at the brown water of the Mississippi River drifting far below and thought for a moment of turning back. She tried to see the other women's faces in the rear-view mirror; she wanted to tell them she had changed her mind. Then she remembered her pledge to John Wisdom and squelched her fears.

It wasn't difficult to find the school, since Belle Chasse, a dreary town, had only one street—the highway that ran through it. Other than the school and a few plantations, the town existed mostly for the large naval base located there. Ruth had been told that most of the children who attended the school came from families temporarily stationed at Belle Chasse. Ruth parked the car in the empty courtyard in front of the school and got out to hold her umbrella open. Helen and Renna crowded under it with Ruth while Blondie and Mathilde shared another umbrella. Fumbling their way up the path sideways like crabs, they climbed the concrete steps and entered the new brick building. They shook the rain from their coats, removed their galoshes, and found an empty coat rack in the teachers' room. There they left their wet things and their bags of sandwiches. The heavy rain probably was a good thing, Ruth thought grimly, for if the sun had been out, maybe some of the townspeople might have come out, too. Angry mobs had thrown stones in other school districts.

As they closed the door of the teachers' room, the principal of the school finally came out of her office, looked at her watch, and pointed the way to the classrooms. Then she turned and went back to her desk. The women had already decided that Mathilde would take the first grade and Ruth the third. The other classrooms would be combined, depending on the number of children. They agreed on a time for lunch and parted.

When Ruth opened the door of her classroom she was greeted with fifteen empty desks, a barren bulletin board, a locked closet, and a teacher's desk with all its empty drawers hanging out like hungry mouths. How would she spend the next two weeks teaching these children without any materials? Her face flushed with anger, but she tried to control herself as she and the others marched down to the principal to demand some supplies. Wearing a broad smile, the principal told them that no teaching materials were available. Apparently, Perez had given everything—even the student books—to the segregated academies that had sprouted up in nearby Algiers. Ruth had encountered polite smiles on the faces of school principals accustomed to dealing with problems; but she was unable to read this smile and interpret which side the woman was on. They would just have to be creative, Ruth decided.

When she returned to the classroom, Ruth noticed that even the flag was missing. "It's a wonder they didn't replace it with the Confederate one," she thought bitterly, as she turned to write her name, Miss Dreyfous, in her neatest penmanship on the blackboard. "Lucky I have one piece of chalk," she commented to the silent walls.

As soon as she heard the sounds of children, Ruth went to the door to greet them. Although she had never taught in a regular classroom, for many years Ruth had administered group tests to classes and had led discussions with children in her capacity as psychologist and guidance director at Newman School. Besides, she felt confident that she knew how to talk to children. It wasn't long before the students found their seats and waited for her to begin. Ruth looked in amazement at the room full of children; not one place was empty. It seemed that Perez' threats had not kept the children away from school, after all. She started with geography. "What country are you studying?" she asked them. When they told her that their last lesson had been on Greece, Ruth drew a rather primitive outline of that country on the blackboard. As she talked and drew, the children journeyed with her as she described all the classical sights she had visited on trips through Greece. She drew the Acropolis, the Temple of Athena at Delphi, and the theater at Epidaurus. Recalling myths about gods and heroes, she spun tales for them. Ruth gave them her crash course in culture.

The day passed quickly as she engulfed them in a vast stream that flowed from her own sources of knowledge and experience. They listened to her descriptions, responded when she asked them questions, and earnestly tried to figure out the problems she generated on the board during arithmetic time. Shortly after the children finished lunch, an energetic romp around the gym, and a rest time at their desks, dismissal time was signaled by the bell.

Ruth had made it through day one. The rain had stopped, but still no one had protested or tried to interfere. Ruth was pleased to learn from some of the mothers who had come for their children that most of the naval base personnel, many of whom were not from Louisiana, had vowed to cooperate with integration. At a meeting the night before, they had voted to support any effort to keep the school open, which explained the children's perfect attendance. Ruth was pleased that she had come.

Once in the car, the five women shared experiences and tried to help one another plan for the next two weeks of teaching. Renna had not said a word, but as they crossed over the bridge to New Orleans, she confessed that she would not be returning the next day because she had been told not to come back. Apparently, her zealous lecture to the children on human rights and integration had been piped into the principal's office over the intercom. Renna had been fired from her first and only job as volunteer teacher. They would have to find someone to replace her in the fourth grade.

Somehow, the other women managed to keep the children's attention and to create lessons for two weeks. Their names were printed in the New Orleans newspapers, but although they received a few angry anonymous calls at their homes, no one interrupted their teaching or tried to abuse or harass them physically. No incident occurred like the one George experienced when he had been kicked and shoved by angry women. A few people they knew called to express concern that anti-Semitism might spread, since the White Citizens Council hated Jews as much as Negroes: they knew Ruth and Mathilde were Jewish—and, of course, George had already been blacklisted some years before. But Ruth was unconcerned.

The last day that they taught in Belle Chasse, the children brought cookies and juice to the school. Even the principal came out of her office to join the party. Ruth was sad to leave the children after those two weeks, but as the women made ready to drive away, they saw several pickup trucks pull into the courtyard. Not only were the teachers returning, but they had also found a way to rescue some of the materials and books. Ruth felt glad that she had helped save this little school—at least for now—and perhaps their victory would spur others to fight and win. Her fingers tightened around the car steering wheel as she thought about the other women who had refused to come. As mothers, perhaps they worried too much about the possible dangers. Ruth had no regrets. She believed she had made the right choice in going to Belle Chasse: teaching those children and feeling appreciated for having defeated the bigots satisfied her.

Why, she wondered, had she agreed to sell Audubon Place, her father's home, to a member of the Perez family? . . .

When Ruth finished her story, she extended her pale, blue-veined hand and groped for her iced coffee as Alma came to take away the near-empty glass. Alma held it to her lips so she could sip the last drops. After the tray was removed from the coffee table, I rearranged the displaced photographs—the crowded gallery of her newest angels. I thought about her story and wondered if I would have had the courage to place myself in that dangerous situation. Her convictions led her to act, and I felt proud of her. In the fading light I saw her hands begin again to rub each other as she sat back in her chair. Her next words startled me; her mind had shifted to another topic, leaving me still pondering her role in the fight for school integration.

"Yes, I had several opportunities, but there was no one I wanted to marry. Well, there was one . . . on one of my trips to Europe. I met him on the boat. . . . He was going to get off in Italy, but he stayed on the cruise to be with me. He followed me to Florence and then London . . . but he was married, had children, and I couldn't do that—break up a family. . . . No, I let him go."

I wanted to ask more about this romance, since I had not heard this story before, but evening darkened the room, shutting out the last shadows beneath the oak tree in the garden and silencing her willing reminiscing. Impatiently she called for dinner to be served.

As we mopped with bits of French bread the last drops of rich brown gravy from the crawfish stew, the conversation turned to contemporary events: the approaching local election as well as national and foreign affairs. Even without the ability to read, Ruth keeps current by listening to news programs and having the entire Sunday New York *Times* read to her. Reminding her that we'd be back in the morning, we finished the last cup of coffee and prepared to leave. I had invited her to take me to visit the cemetery on Elysian Fields Avenue where her grandparents were buried; I wanted also to see the house my great-grandparents once lived in on Esplanade Avenue, and I hoped we'd have time to see once again my grandparents' house on Audubon Place, Ruth's former home.

Early that next morning, when Alby and I arrived at her gate, she was dressed in a blue cotton suit and red-checked blouse, ready for the journey. Despite two surgeries in the past year, one for a broken hip and the other for a malignant tumor, Ruth moved with surprising agility into the front seat of the car, and the three of us began our journey.

Alby and I had found no spare time to wander the Quarter or shop for pralines, as we usually do when we come to New Orleans, so I detoured a few blocks through the Quarter before heading for our destination. As usual, jean-clad tourists roamed the streets carrying half-empty plastic glasses of beer, and I wasn't surprised that Bourbon Street seemed more gaudy at ten in the morning than at midnight, with sun lighting the faces, legs, and bare breasts of women on faded posters plastered on the sides of open doorways of seedy bars. Loud Dixieland music blasted forth and followed us as we continued on past souvenir shop windows crowded with tee-shirts and coffee mugs painted with New Orleans motifs — tipsy lamp-posts, alligators, and saxophones. Leaving the tourist streets behind, we followed the route the old streetcar named Desire once took to Elysian Fields.

"Find Esplanade first," Ruth commanded. "Turn left and you will see my grandfather Abel's house."

"How will I know it?" I asked, wondering how, without full vision, she could tell me.

"There's a monument on the neutral ground — a fountain of some sort, and the house is on a corner, on the left," she explained, confident that I could follow her directions.

We drove past tree-shaded homes with large grounds, once owned by French settlers who had lived on this quiet street in elegant houses, but now the homes show signs of neglect. No longer a Creole neighborhood, new residents have transformed the homes into boardinghouses, and lawns and gardens no longer are planted with grass and flowers. I expected Ruth to tell me to stop at one of these, but we drove on, the houses becoming smaller and smaller. With her uncanny memory for places and her instinct for knowing distances, Ruth informed me we were not yet there.

"Pretty soon you'll see the monument, then turn and you'll see the house."

Just as she said this I saw a mound of stones on the neutral ground—probably the statue—but no large home in sight. I saw a cottage—a small yellow house with shuttered windows, built right out to the edge of the sidewalk. When I described this unimposing structure, she exclaimed that we had found it.

"Ruth, it's so small! How in the world did they live here with all those children? Did they always live in this house?"

"Oh, it goes way back and there's a second story back there," she explained with a curt tone, but I could not see it. The etched lead glass in the heavy, paneled front door whispered my great-grandfather's proud beginnings—the arrival of Abel Dreyfous in America.

"Mother and Father lived here, too, when they were first married. They were called back from their honeymoon when Abel died, and they settled in this house with Caroline. It was so hot in their bedroom on the top floor, the paint on their bedroom furniture blistered."

I never knew that my grandparents, Julia and Felix, had begun their married life here in this little house before moving on to Jackson Avenue, where American families lived, and then further uptown to Audubon Place, near Tulane, not far from the Dominican Street home where I grew up. I looked down the street at the shabby houses and tried to envision a lively French community living here as new immigrants in a city far away from France. It didn't match the image of the Creole neighborhood I envisioned from my reading of Kate Chopin's novel *The Awakening*. I opened the car door, stood in front of the house, and entered the nineteenth-century world of my great-grandparents.

10

Abel Dreyfous:
January, 1849

$\mathscr{A}$s Abel Dreyfous walked down Esplanade toward his notarial office, he thought about the letter in his pocket. He wondered if he
ought to post it, for he knew he sounded despondent; he wanted the letter
to help ease his sister Josephine's pain, not reflect the lonely mood of a
widower of thirty-four. Abel felt her grief at losing a child and wished he
could go to her to comfort her, but France was far away, and he had troubles
of his own. As he walked slowly, feeling tired from heat as intense as that
of France in July, worry and grief crushed his spirit: the loss of his wife,
Alice, and the responsibility for their two young children engulfed him. He
longed for his sister and for France.

Although he had lived in New Orleans for ten years, he believed he
would never grow accustomed to the hot weather. At least here, in this
country, he was free to apprentice and then become a notary, even open his
own office. Well, now, he thought, at least I'm not still in New York working
in dry goods or trying to succeed with the soap factory as I did when first
I came to New Orleans . . . and, thank the Lord, the cholera epidemic seems
over. He felt some relief from that worry—about his two little girls' health
and his own, what with two thousand people having died over the past six
weeks. He had written to his sister, "What would have become of them
without me—especially having recently lost their mother, my dear wife?"
Abel wondered why he had conveyed his dreary thoughts to poor Josephine,
who had just lost her young daughter, Emilie. At the end of the letter, he
made an attempt to comfort her: "She died young with all her illusions,

before knowing the pains, the miseries, and the sufferings of life. Console yourself, *ma chère soeur*," he had written. "Accept the decrees of Providence." Abel knew his words reflected his own grief, and he asked himself if he could follow his own wise counsel.

Even though cholera cases had diminished, Abel wondered when he'd feel secure and free from worry. So many people had left the city during the scare, and most offices were still closed. Yes, he thought, "when fear is in the heart, one does not think of business." But now he had to find a way to recuperate his financial losses. He hurried his pace despite the heat. He would stop at a café for a demi-tasse and read his letters again before going to the office.

The other letter in Abel's pocket, addressed to his mother-in-law, expressed his despair, but the tone of the letter reflected his spirit of optimism, especially in the final paragraphs, where he described California: "Gold is found in all the rivers, in all the streams. . . . Hordes of adventurers transport themselves to this new El Dorado. . . . I must admit that if I did not have two children and a sure position here I would go to that country, not to prospect for gold in the sand, but I would bring a good deal of merchandise which certainly would bring me a profit several hundred times its original value."

Abel wondered when he would see his family in France again. How strange that his daughters had never met their grandmothers or aunts. He talked about them to his children every day and tried to teach them to love their relatives even before meeting them. Abel closed his eyes as he sipped his coffee, trying to see the faces that he had left behind in Alsace ten years ago, trying also to visualize the quiet village of Belfort, his home, the synagogue, and the cemetery where his grandfather, Judas, and his father, Emanuel, lay under plain stone markers he had often stood before. Abel never knew his grandfather and barely remembered his own father, who had died before Abel was five. But his mother, Rose. . . . He could see her sweet face, pale and drawn, framed in the black silk she always wore. If only, he thought, I could see her again.

The days passed slowly that year as Abel tried to grow accustomed to awakening each morning in the emptiness of the room he had once shared with his wife. Instead of dining at home alone, however, he preferred late-night suppers at a small restaurant on Toulouse Street, in the company of a colleague or client. After kissing the children good-night, he'd meet his companion, first order oysters, then tournadot, and after finishing crème anglaise and demitasse, the men would linger over a bottle of wine, discussing the cotton business and the news from France.

During the first few years in America, he'd been strict about obeying the old dietary laws, but he compromised now by keeping kosher only at home. Life had been different in France, because all his close associates were Jewish. Keeping the traditions seemed complicated in America, where he sometimes dined in mixed company. He believed that some of the old ways would soon change.

During dinner one balmy evening, a Jewish client, a good friend with whom he had dined several times, persuaded Abel to call on his cousin's daughter. This man had made the suggestion the week before, but Abel had demurred. The idea of courting made him feel uncomfortable—especially paying a call on a girl so young—and so soon . . . with memories of Alice still intense. But his daughters . . . he ought to think of them.

After several afternoons of visiting in her parlor, Abel proposed marriage to Caroline Kaufman. With the approval of her father, they became engaged and shortly thereafter were married in a little synagogue named Temime Derech (The Right Way). It didn't take long for his daughters, Cecile and Alice, to grow fond of their new mother, and once again Abel looked forward to coming home to the house on Esplanade Avenue.

Over the next few years, the painful memory of the death of Abel's first wife, Alice, faded. When he walked to his office in the morning, Caroline's face, her happy smile, lingered in his mind—her image restored him, giving him back his former spirit. He felt alive and able to excel in his work. He was proud of the way Caroline performed her duties as wife and mother and was especially pleased when she presented him with a son, Emile, born in 1851, a year after they were married.

Caroline gave birth to eight more children during these first sixteen years of her marriage. Emile was followed by Amalie, then Anna, Felix, and Jules. Charles, who was born in 1865, died at two years old of yellow fever while Caroline labored in the next room, giving birth to Martha, who also died in infancy. Caroline and Abel struggled over the years as their family expanded. Luckily, they could afford one slave to help with the household chores. Abel had wrestled with his conscience when he purchased the young serving girl, but Caroline seemed weary and hardly able to get up in the morning, especially after losing Charles, and he worried about her. Thinking of Alice, terror filled his heart when he saw Caroline's drawn and pallid countenance, but with her exceptional resilience her spirits soon returned, and she resumed her motherly duties along with her cheerful temperament.

More difficult times followed, however, during the war years and the long period of Reconstruction. The family faced food and clothing shortages, but they managed to do without some of what they once considered necessities. No longer could they afford a servant to help with the housework and care of the children. Businesses all over the city came to a standstill, and Abel struggled to earn enough from his law practice so he would not have to dip into investments.

He thought there would be no more babies but Caroline gave birth to another girl. When she arrived, Abel, still mourning his mother's death the year before, gave this baby his mother's name, Rose. Even though Abel now could shake off the dark moods that used to envelop him before he married Caroline, it saddened him each time he looked at this child, whose face Abel's own mother would never see. If only he could return to Paris, to see his sisters and visit his mother's grave in Belfort, but writing served as the only link with his family in France for thirty-five years. When Caroline gave birth to yet another little girl, Blanche, he knew he'd have to push aside any thoughts of leaving her and the children—even though he could afford to go now that business had improved somewhat. Soon I'll go, he resolved.

July, 1874

Finally, in July, 1874, Abel planned his journey. First he'd visit his brothers, his married daughter Anna, and other relatives in New York. Later he'd book passage on the steamer to see at last his family in France. He felt it was possible now to have his long-awaited reunion. Political and economic conditions in the South had improved somewhat, although some of the sufferings of Reconstruction lingered. Now, for the first time, he could hop aboard a railroad car and reach New York in only a few days. Then, too, he knew he could leave Caroline alone, since their children, who were mostly grown now, no longer needed constant attention. He wished he could take her with him, but she was still needed at home. Abel hated leaving her to swelter in the July heat of New Orleans, but Caroline wanted him to go, insisting only that he write long letters with detailed descriptions so she could share his experiences. For weeks she prepared for his journey: washing, pressing, mending, sewing, and packing his trunk. The day he left for the station, she had packed a ponderous basket of food: hard-boiled eggs, roasted chicken, breads, and fruit. She held back her tears until his carriage turned the corner away from Esplanade, but she wiped them quickly before going inside.

Three days, six hard-boiled eggs, a few light suppers in the dining wagon, and one roasted chicken thigh later, the train screeched to the station platform on the New Jersey side of the Hudson River. Waiting there on the platform was his daughter Anna with her husband, Bernard Fellman. After greeting him, Anna laughed at the soot and dirt from the smoke of the locomotive that covered her meticulous father's face and white shirt.

"Come, Father, we'll have to bathe you several times to make you presentable," Anna teased. "Let's go—we have plans that will take up the whole afternoon and take you all over Manhattan."

Abel gazed in wonder at the sights of the city as they explored New York that afternoon. Dizzy from the clatter of carriages and the hurried pace of New York, he sought peace in Central Park, which he thought must be the Garden of Eden. The stores and offices of the business district astonished him, but he was most overwhelmed by the houses people lived in, when compared to his little house in the French Quarter. After dinner, back in his room at Mrs. Stern's, he wrote to Caroline and the children, "This house, by the way, is a real palace, worth over $44,000. . . . If you want to have an idea of comfort you must see how the houses are equipped here—hot and cold water, bathroom and toilet on each floor, and all this built with a luxury unknown to our poor Southern regions."

The next afternoon he met his two nephews, Raphael and Isidore, sons of his sister Jeannette, who helped him book passage for France on the S.S. Washington. That night, his brother Joseph's son and daughter (Henry and Cecilia Springer) treated him to a concert in Central Park. Abel sat between Cecilia's two young daughters, Linda and Anna; but in spite of the joyful sounds of music and the look of delight on the children's faces, Abel felt perturbed about his afternoon encounter with his younger brother Simeon and about seeing Emilie, Simeon's blind daughter. After the concert, alone in his room, he wrote Caroline about this experience: "I rushed back of my brother and tapped him on the shoulder. . . . I found him changed to his disadvantage, and his memory often fails him since his stroke. . . . We went to my brother's house . . . which I did not like at all although it cost $15,000. It is only 17 feet wide and has only one opening on the street besides the entrance door. It is three stories high, but I would suffocate in those narrow and dark rooms. . . . I climbed up [to the third floor] and faced a poor blind girl, pale, her hair cut short and looking like a boy. She welcomed me smiling and said: 'I have never seen you, Uncle, yet I know and love you.' . . . I could not refrain from crying." Simeon's bitterness and selfishness angered Abel, yet he felt Simeon cared for him. Perhaps, he thought, I'm the only person for whom he has any affection.

The next morning Abel woke early to bathe and pack the last items in his trunk, for the steamer was leaving at twelve-thirty. His daughter Anna and Mrs. Springer drove him to the depot in their carriage. When they arrived at the gangplank of the steamer, they found all the members of his family already there. Once aboard, Isidore and Raphael ordered champagne to toast him and wish him bon voyage. Abel marveled at the size of the steamship and the luxurious cabin he'd been assigned. The seas were calm for the eleven days of the voyage.

When the ship docked in Brest, he posted a letter home to his family commenting that "there is no hotel in the world where one can be more comfortable. Each meal was a real banquet. . . . My trip would have been the best in the world if I had with me my dear wife and at least my little Blanchette . . . how much Mama would have enjoyed the food."

Eleven days at sea seem relatively short compared with a thirty-five-year separation from family and boyhood home, yet Abel's impatience must have made the days seem long. At least, unlike travel today, he arrived rested— no jet lag for him. I find it strange, however, that his shipboard letters did not reflect the emotions he must have felt as the ship steamed toward France. Rather than writing about his feelings of anticipation, he appeared to have as his letter-writing purpose the reporting of his experiences in detail: by describing his observations of the sumptuous meals and the people he met, he could have his family enjoy his trip vicariously. Or, possibly, Abel simply left his intense emotions unexpressed. As he said himself in a subsequent letter, feelings are easier to imagine than to describe. Even though I was moved by his vivid descriptions of Paris, by his enthusiasm for the homes of his family, and by his impressions of people, I wished he had written more about how he felt as he approached those shores again.

La Belle France

After disembarking in Le Havre, Abel made arrangements for his trunks to be shipped, and boarded the train for the five-hour journey to Paris. He was overjoyed to see his sister Josephine after thirty-five years. He found her children perfect, and they were happy to have him visit. Her daughter Caroline felt weak and sick from the first stages of her fifth pregnancy, but she visited every day. Some days, she brought her four children: the three-and-a-half-year-old Emile, the two babies, and the younger boy, Marcel—who everyone thought looked like Abel's son Felix. Abel looked forward to seeing Josephine's other daughter, Adele Somers, and her daughter, Adeline.

As he drove through the streets of Paris, Abel thought, "There is only one Paris; no other city could be compared to it. . . . What beautiful parks and what beautiful landscapes." So many invitations, so many dinners and people to see that Abel felt exhausted, but it was such a joy to be so welcomed by all his family and old friends, who lived in tasteful homes. He was impressed with Josephine's son Adolphe's country house outside Paris at Billancourt; it made him wonder why he had ever left France, if a man could earn so much money here.

As he described Paris and the comfortable homes of his family in these letters, I detected a tinge of regret for having made the decision to leave France for America. When he was a newcomer to America, the tone of his early letters back to his family in France expressed dissatisfaction with his new life—especially the conditions in the South. He conveyed such longing for France that I wondered what led him to leave family and friends for a country he'd never seen. He perhaps thought, like many young men in those days, that America promised more opportunity than his native land, and he probably brushed aside the thoughts of never seeing some of his family again. The spirit of adventure and the possibility of making a fortune lured him; or else wars, politics, and anti-Semitism in Europe forced his decision to leave. Although America didn't live up to his expectations, once he established himself, he couldn't return. Now back in France, he was struck with regret and melancholy when he realized so many family members had died; some of them he'd never met. He had missed sharing with his sisters those times of grief. Thus, despite the thrill of returning home to France, hearing his native language, and being in familiar places, coming home after the long separation generated pleasure but also much pain. I hear his ambivalence when I read his letters from France.

One day, on a walk through the Bois de Boulogne with his sister Jeannette's son George, he listened as George talked about deceased relatives Abel had never met. It grieved him to think about these close family members, and he sighed when he thought about his sisters Caroline and Adelaide, who had died a few years ago. He thought once again of his first wife, Alice, buried so far away from France. He found it difficult to cope with the melancholy that weighed on him as he thought how time and distance had wrenched apart the bonds of family.

The next evening Abel had dinner at Fontenay, in the country home of Captain Meyer, the widower of his sister Josephine's deceased daughter, Cecile. Adelaide's daughter, Selina, also lived there, caring for the two motherless little girls, Madelaine and Marcel. When he looked at them, it saddened him to remember that their grandmother, his sister Caroline, and their mother, his niece, were both dead. In his weekly letter home, Abel expressed his shock that Selina, a single woman, lived alone in a widower's home. He voiced concern for his niece's reputation. But, alas, he admitted in his letter, this is France . . . and perhaps I've forgotten the difference between French attitudes and those in America I've become accustomed to. He confessed how much he had enjoyed the dancing girls he had seen the night before. "How beautiful and graceful they were! Such pretty clothes— that is to say, almost no clothes. It was an enchantment, but the truth obliges me to admit that it was indecent."

After three weeks in Paris, Abel arrived in Belfort, the place where he grew up, the city he had longed to see for thirty-five years. I can imagine the agitation he felt as he stood once again in the place he had dreamed of for so many years. I know when I return to New Orleans after being away how strange it feels to go back: when I first arrive, it's like entering a part of myself again—the child that I left behind. I want to feel it's home, but it's changed, and so have I.

Abel wanted once again to feel at home in the familiar Alsatian city nestled beneath the ruins of a fort, on the red cliff rising sharply above the Hôtel de Ville. Instead, he wrote Caroline that he felt "sadness and a deep nostalgia . . . remembering all the dead and seeing a place where I had become a stranger and could not recognize . . . the extraordinary enlarge-ment of its area and of its population, its happy activity and animation." And, thank God, he thought, at least Belfort has never been a German city, unlike other places in Alsace. Miraculously, Belfort never fell under German rule.

For hours he walked the streets looking for remembered landmarks, just as I feel compelled to find places special to me in New Orleans when I go back. I revisit the same scenes of my childhood each time I go, so that I can connect them with pictures from my memory. Like an artist restoring a fading oil painting, I need to retouch my images of Louisiana and make them bright again. I am drawn to see the park, the river, trees, and buildings, even though some have changed beyond recognition. I can't imagine coming home after being away as long as Abel and trying to find familiarity.

Later that same day, he visited the Hebrew Cemetery in the Jewish section, away from the old section of the city. On the way he searched for his house, the place where he was born; but the neighborhood had changed so much, he couldn't even find the *boulangerie* on the corner where his mother shopped for fresh rolls each morning, and even the streets had changed their names. Thoroughly lost, he walked on, winding his way up the hill to the cemetery.

What draws us to cemeteries, he thought, as he wandered through the markers with all the names of deceased Dreyfous family members he had known and loved. Why do we feel the compulsion to visit the dead and stir up old memories that sadden us? In some way, he reflected, connecting with those who have passed on gives us a sense of who we are and tells us something of the journey we've been on—maybe when we come to cemeteries, we can fathom where death will take us in the end. We stand at the foot of graves, trying to envision the person beneath, as if those remains can tell us about ourselves—tell us how they made us what we are. Or, he thought, perhaps we come to feel the finality of death, to cry and be done forever with grieving. He remembered the site he had chosen for his own grave, the Hebrew Rest Cemetery on Elysian Fields Avenue in New Orleans, where Alice and the babies already lay waiting for him.

Down a hill near the fence under a vine-covered stone, he read his father's and mother's names and tried once again to recall their faces and hear their voices call his name. He thought of his daughter Rose, the child back home his mother never saw, and knelt down to kiss the same name, etched there in the stone that marks the earth that covers his mother's remains—his mother for whom he named his little girl.

Living far away from my own mother, I know the pain of separation and what grief he must have felt for having been away so long—not seeing her over the years as she aged—and knowing that she missed him more and more as she grew weak and lonely. Each time I visit Mother, I fear departing, not knowing when I'll return, and I despair at leaving her alone. How distraught he must have been, for he had never had the chance to bid her farewell or touch her hand before she died.

But, he remembered, he had come to see the living. He wanted to visit his childhood friends and to enjoy the beautiful Alsatian country with its abundant orchards and vineyards. In his letter home to his family, Abel described how "trees are bent down by the weight of the fruit; wine merchants do not know where to find enough barrels for their wine . . . and among other remarkable things [I saw] a single vine which bore over 1100 bunches of grapes."

After tearing himself away from Belfort, Abel traveled to Colmar, to Mulhouse, through the medieval villages along the wine route to Strasbourg, and then returned to Paris. In Paris once again, Abel spent his days purchasing clothes for himself, watches for Jules and Felix, and fine materials to take home to Caroline and the children. Adolphe and Jules, Josephine's two sons, helped him with his shopping. Abel wrote to Felix that Jules's wife was very pretty and that "he received 30,000 francs" when they were married, but even though Adolphe could have a "fine fiancée and a fine dowry any day . . . he does not want to leave his family." To his son,

Abel wrote, "Boy, when you come in 1876, if you are courteous and have good manners, you will be able to choose here a very pretty woman. . . . Their dowries will bring you plenty of money."

Abel wanted to buy Caroline a black hat with poppies or cherries or daisies that he saw in a fancy Parisian shop, but he couldn't make up his mind which to buy and decided instead on a gray linen dress with white embroidery and tunic. He also purchased a dark-blue silk dress with a matching vest, but then he returned to the store and bought the hat with daisies. When he returned to his room, Abel wrote to his wife, "How many beautiful things I have seen, and what good fruit I have eaten: cherries, plums, grapes, melons, pears, peaches, and everything so cheap! If only I could have you here."

During his last few days in Paris, Abel made a final effort to locate his sister Jeannette, for he had not yet seen her. To his delight, he found her husband, who told him she would be arriving in Paris that afternoon. They hurried to the station, and as they helped Jeannette and her daughter off the train, she looked at Abel with surprise, wondering who he was. "Don't you recognize me?" Abel asked Jeannette, but she shook her head. "Then I told her that I had come from America, from New Orleans."

"You are my brother Abel!" she cried out. She had not recognized him, because she'd been only nine when he had left France.

The only family member Abel did not see was Emile, who had become, as Abel phrased it in his letter, the "greatest enemy of his parents and his brothers. . . . He is ruled by his concubine, a very bad woman. . . . This must be the reason he has not made any great efforts to meet me."

Abel's last letters home were filled with details of his purchases and his efforts to crowd his last days in France with all he could see and do before leaving. Knowing that he'd be separated once again, he seemed unable to commit himself to a particular departure date, even though he longed to see his wife and children. He knew he must soon book his passage and prepare to leave.

September arrived. Abel was eager for home but thought he would re-main in Paris for Rosh Hashanah—even though it would be his first time away from his wife during this season. He also wanted to stay to attend the consecration of the new temple in Paris, which the newspapers described as a magnificent building. The day after the ceremony, Abel clipped the articles describing the new temple and enclosed them in an envelope with his last letter home. In it, he expressed the conflicting emotions he had felt throughout the journey: his unbounded enthusiasm for all the material and natural wonders he saw often became overcast by his longing for home and family. He wrote, "I count the days when we will be reunited. . . . I shall never leave again without taking my big wife. . . . Nothing amuses or distracts me; yet there are still so many fine things to see." Before packing all his new shirts and gifts into his trunk, he bought some baby clothes to bring back to Anna, and on September 25, Abel sailed for home.

$\mathcal{F}$inale

I took one long last look at the little yellow house and imagined my great-grandfather living here, loving his family yet yearning for France and those he had left behind. I tried to imagine his leaving his family as a youth, traveling so far when distances could be crossed solely by slow-moving ships, and only returning to France after thirty-five years had passed. Without telephones or planes, separation meant being out of touch for weeks. I wonder if Abel's courage, spirit, and stoicism was a Dreyfous characteristic, which he passed on to Felix and to Felix's children.

I also thought about my great-grandmother Caroline as a young woman living in Louisiana during the last half of the nineteenth century. What strength she must have had, marrying at sixteen, nurturing so many children, caring for their needs, and grieving for those who died in infancy. From the patronizing tone in which Abel often wrote to her, I thought of Edna Pontellier, the woman married to a Creole in Kate Chopin's novel *The Awakening*. I know that in nineteenth-century Louisiana the Napoleonic Code declared women the property of their husbands, with limited rights to land and legal decisions, and because that document placed women in the same category as children, their husbands often treated them in a condescending manner. Although Edna rebelled when she awakened to a recognition of other desires, it appears that Caroline submitted to Abel's commands, accepted his admonishments, and played well the role of "mother-woman." It would take two generations more for women to see themselves in other guises.

Ruth's call from the automobile reminded me that we still had places to see on our journey that morning. After taking a few photographs of the house and the street, I returned to the car and, with Ruth's directions, found the old Hebrew Rest Cemetery, the second stop on our itinerary. I helped Ruth out of the car and held her arm as she, without seeing, pointed to the site of her grandparents' graves. Pushing her walker, she led us under the ornate cast-iron archway, through the rows of raised tombs until we found ourselves standing in front of Abel and Caroline's grave. In all the years that I lived in New Orleans, I had never visited this site. Standing there this day, I could barely make out the names or the dates on the tall marker at the center of the plot, because the wind and the rain had washed away some of the letters, but the simple headstones, one etched with the word MÈRE, and the other with PÈRE, were clear. Under these stones lay the remains of Caroline and Abel Dreyfous.

I thought of Abel's visit to the cemetery in Belfort, seeing his mother's grave for the first time. Although I never knew Abel, I felt a spiritual closeness to him as if this marker made him real. I, too, had visited the cemetery in Belfort one summer on a pilgrimage there. The day was hot, the weeds had grown high, and many of the graves had been desecrated by the Nazis, but with the help of an aged sexton and a book listing the plots, we found the graves of Abel's family—my ancestors. I felt a bridge back over time as I stood looking at those tortured stones.

I again looked at Caroline's marker with the single word MÈRE, and I pictured her with her brood, bustling about in the little yellow house, waiting patiently while her husband traveled through France. I wondered whether Caroline ever had the chance to take a journey back to Demmelsdorf, Germany, where her grandfather Julius Goodhart was born, or to Messelfeld, Germany, the birthplace of her grandmother, Rosa Rosenbaum. I don't believe she even traveled with Abel to Paris to choose her own hat on the Champs-Elysées.

My mother (named for her grandmothers, Caroline Seeman and Caroline Dreyfous) never knew her grandfather Abel, for he died in 1892 before Ruth and Mother were born. But Abel's wife Caroline lived with my grandparents, Felix and Julia, in their house on Jackson Avenue until she died. When my mother was a little girl, her room adjoined her grandmother's room, and each night at bedtime, Mother tiptoed into Caroline's room, kissed her, and said, "*Bon soir, Mama, dormez bien.*"

I thought of these words as I stood in the cemetery that afternoon. What do I know of this woman who gave birth every two years—ten births, I believe, in less than two decades of married life. A woman who stayed at home most of her life, whose letters—if she wrote any—were not preserved? How did she respond when Emile, her oldest son, left home to work on the Panama Canal, abandoned his wife and children, and never returned? Is it only a coincidence that she died in 1914, the same year the canal was completed? Maybe Abel told her Emile was "away," keeping his disappearance and whereabouts a secret from her; she never knew about his new Hispanic family. Nor did we until recently, when a cousin from Salt Lake City sent pictures of Dreyfous families living in Bogota, Colombia, and in Santo Domingo—descendants of Emile Dreyfous. Perhaps to erase his existence, his name never was mentioned by anyone again: did Abel also believe that silence wipes away memory and smothers grief and pain? Not speaking about dreadful events appears to be a family trait.

I looked at the second large marker with the name Charles and wondered how often Caroline came here to grieve for her two-year-old son who died in 1867 or for the baby girl whose name I could not find engraved on a headstone. Pains when giving birth, when burying a child, when abandoned by a husband or children, were events that women suffered alone—often in silence. Seeing the child Charles' grave made me think of Daddy's baby son Teddy, and I wondered where he lies buried. How quickly the memory of him vanished because no one spoke his name. There are no family photographs of him—or his mother whom grief destroyed.

I was reminded of the portrait in my mother's living room—that woman dressed in black with hair brushed back, sitting with shoulders square, without a smile on her stern face. When I was a child, that harsh face frightened me; now I see that the stony face may reflect her endurance, her courage and strength, and not a mean spirit. Although her portrait has been hanging for many years in the living room, my mother couldn't remember her name when I asked her this morning. She told me it might be Abel's first wife, or the first wife of Abel's father—Hannah Lévy. Whoever's wife or mother she was, the woman in this painting's voicelessness made her anonymous and easily replaced if she died in childbearing years, as so many women did. Since she made no significant contributions outside of the home that written documents confirm or that our culture values, her name no longer is spoken.

Yet, in silence her face speaks to me. I like to think she's a composite of all the women in the family I have written about—each one strong in a different way. She is Caroline Dreyfous, my great-grandmother—kind, submissive, quiet, and steadfast—much like her daughter-in-law, my grandmother Julia. Ruth bears a resemblance to the face in the portrait, for her strength is her defiance, intelligence, independence, and vision. My mother, Caroline, who sits in her mechanized chair beneath this painting, has none of that woman's physical features, for there is tranquility in Mother's face despite her forceful temperament and her encounter with catastrophe. She dared marry the man she loved, having overcome her parents' objections, just as later she overcame in silent courage Daddy's tragic fall. The men in the family forged success and power; the women invented for themselves the roles they played.

As Ruth, Alby, and I retraced our steps through the silent stones of the Hebrew Rest Cemetery, suddenly the name Weiss, marking a grassy plot several feet away, shouted out at me. Leaving the main path, I climbed over some stones and stopped and stared at the grave of my father's parents: Theodore Weiss and Lena Silverstein Weiss—the grandparents I never knew—and Sidney Weiss, Daddy's younger brother—never mentioned as far as I remember, except that Daddy's nephew Sidney must have been named after him.

Here was the headstone that my father designed for his parents, with the same clean lines and plain face that Mother had copied for Daddy's grave. A graceful spray of ivy carved above their names softened the boxy structure. Then I saw two single rays from the setting sun cast an eerie bright streak across the grass, forming two yellow lines on the dark green grass above the remains of my grandparents—my father's mother and father—and an uncle, all strangers to me.

I have only fragments about their lives, for no strong women on my father's side of the family are left to tell me their stories—except for my first cousin, Doris Weiss Weiller, my father's niece, and her sister-in-law, Margaret Weiss Silver. My father's nephew, Doris' brother Sidney, died of polio in an epidemic soon after his marriage. No one knows what happened to his young family. All that I know about my paternal grandfather, Theodore Weiss, is that he was born in Ingwiller, a charming little Alsatian village with hardly a trace remaining today of a once-thriving Jewish community. Tom Schwab, Mathilde Dreyfous' son, told me that some of his father's family came from that same town, and some of them survived the Holocaust by dodging Nazi storm troopers in Vichy France; others died tragically in concentration camps along with millions of other European Jews.

But all that remains in Alsace of the Weiss ancestors are graves in the Hebrew cemetery and records of their births and deaths in the city archives, dating back to Judas Weiss in 1764 and his father, whose name was Isaac Loewel. I thought it strange that his last name wasn't Weiss until someone explained to me that he lived and died before the Napoleonic Code decreed that Jews in France take family names, probably so that the government could add them to the rolls and tax them efficiently. Most likely during this period, the family chose the name Weiss.

Theodore Weiss left Ingwiller and his parents Solomon and Adelle Weiss, settling in Farmerville, Louisiana, where he became an American citizen in 1908 and where my father was born. No one knows why Theodore settled in that rural town, but I'm told that Jews who became peddlers stopped in Cincinnati, were given a route to follow along the Mississippi River, and then some settled in towns along the river and opened stores. Some towns, like Falksville, bear the name of the peddler whose shop became the largest retail outlet in town. The other half-serious explanation for why peddlers like Theodore settled in certain small towns and opened a store was that the town happened to be the place where the horse died, depriving the traveling peddler of his only means of transportation.

Doris, born seventeen years before me, remembers grandfather Theodore as kind and generous—a person everyone liked and a deeply religious man. She also told me that her mother, Estelle Weiss, had a difficult time pleasing her mother-in-law, Lena, who seemed jealous of her son's wives.

Perhaps that resulted from the tragic blow dealt to her in 1867, when she was seven years old. That was the year she and her sisters and brothers— Jonas, age eleven; Caroline, age twelve; Bertha, age five; and Fanny, age three—were placed in the Jewish Children's Home in New Orleans. It was called an asylum in those days, when children of impoverished parents were cared for there. The documents from the home indicate that the Silverstein children were released to older siblings over the years. The oldest son, Charles, who worked in a clothing store, found a position for his younger brother, Jonas, who was released first. Then Lena was discharged to the care of Jonas and her older sister, Carrie. Daddy told Mother that Lena learned dressmaking, earning enough money to support her younger sisters, and enabling the rest of them to be discharged from the home.

Doris' mother, Estelle Weiss, married to Daddy's brother Sol, became a Christian Scientist, hoping to cure her husband of his drinking problem. They and their children, Doris, Saul, and his wife, Margaret, and some of the children converted as well. When they did, the two men changed their names from Saul to Stuart Paul. In the privacy of our family, Daddy always joked about his brother St. Paul. I liked my Uncle Solly and loved our visits to their house. I also liked going down the block to play with Margaret and Saul's children, Teddy and Peggy. I don't remember Doris at all, because she left New Orleans after her wedding in 1935. I haven't seen her since I was three, when I walked down the aisle along with my sister, casting petals from our flower-girl baskets in front of her. To keep with tradition, years later I asked her niece Peggy to be my flower girl.

I looked once more at the silent stone marking the grave of Daddy's parents, and I was startled when I read the short phrase etched below their names, for I had not noticed it when first I gazed. Mother had told me these were Lena's last words, whispered quietly as she died after a lengthy illness in Clifton Springs, New York. Although they are not the same words, for some reason what she uttered reminds me of the closing prayer spoken by the congregation at the close of the Yom Kippur ritual at the end of the long day's fast, just as the last rays of sun disappear from view. My father chose to etch into this stone the last words my grandmother Lena uttered with her dying sigh: "God is love, isn't it wonderful."

Coda

꣠꣠

On the day Franklin Roosevelt's mother died, an ancient oak tree on their land toppled over. What I should have paid attention to when I traveled to New Orleans to celebrate Mother's ninety-seventh birthday last Thanksgiving vacation was not the massive limb of the live oak spreading above but the withering leaves of the hybrid camellia tree in the center of Mother's garden below. I should have known when I saw her that it would be the last time; for now when I look at the photographs of her birthday party, I can see the fatigue and the letting go of her energy that I should have been aware of then. Although she tried to respond to the festivities and to our presence, her spirit had begun its journey to that distant land. Like the variegated camellia bush dying in her garden, she could not bloom another season, but I did not know that. Because I am a child of my mother, I refused to acknowledge weakness or let the thought enter my head that she would ever die. Not now, not ever.

Even though one of the photographs shows a flicker of a smile on her face when one of the new babies bounced on her bed and we stayed up late singing her favorite song, "KKKKatie, beautiful Katie," when I leaned over and kissed her goodbye before our departure the next day and whispered my final "I love you, Mother," she did not reply. She said no goodbye.

What do they mean, these silences? Why did she carry on the family characteristic of hiding despair, fear, and grief from close relations? Why must I rely on photographs to read what we should have spoken about together? She could not speak about death or dying. Did she conceal it from herself, or did she only want to spare me and others from what she was feeling? Call it strength of character, courage, determination, independence, or simply denial.

Two weeks after our visit, the phone call telling me that Mother had slipped away startled me out of my normal routine. After all of her children had visited her one final time, Mother's life ended silently, fitting a pattern consistent with her being, her preferred way of dealing with significant moments. My story ends, and all the threads of my tapestry are broken now. Questions have no primary source for me to query for shreds and patches missing from my tales. What's left of my life on Dominican Street is an empty house waiting to be sold, its contents ready to find a place in other homes.

Although Ruth still lives and can tell more stories about other members of the family, I will never truly finish Mother's tale. I tell Mother's story the way she told it to me with only those truths she wanted others to know. I have tried to add no interpretations or judgments; I have merely colored in details of places I have not visited, events that occurred before my time, and people I never knew.

The night of her funeral I had a dream. Although I know I had been sleeping, the vision I saw seemed so vivid that sometimes now I believe I actually experienced a visitation. In my dream I walked down the back stairs into the kitchen and saw a silver amorphous shape like a mylar cloud, which pulsed as it floated above me. Instinctively, I tried to strike at it as if to make it move away, but it seemed attached to the ceiling light by a thread. It drifted back and pulsated, and when I looked again, it was gone. Although in my dream I saw two of Mother's helpers sitting at the table in the room, I hesitated telling them of my vision, for I knew I would frighten them. Some weeks later, a friend told me Tibetans believe that a soul searches for a body to enter soon after funeral rites are over. Somehow, I felt Mother's presence there in the kitchen that night, hovering above, even though my rational self knows that I dreamed the whole remarkable event. My spiritual being believes that Mother came back, whether in dream or in vision, just as she had from her near-death experience a few years ago. Perhaps she wanted to intervene in my life in some way, assuage my terrible grief. Or did she wish to revise our story, add another piece, or merely reinforce all she wanted me to believe and tell?

I accept her proclamation that the great theme of her life, the love she felt for my father, never faltered. She went to her grave loyal and unbending in her faith in him. His story and hers ends with her steadfast assertion of his innocence. She never allowed a person or tragic event to shatter her spirit or her belief. Caroline and Leon lie together now beneath the stone that bears his name and the inscription that expresses both their lives: *Ad astra per aspera*. To the stars through effort. The rest is silence.

$\mathcal{B}$ibliography

ᵥᵥᵥ

$\mathcal{L}$isted here are works I consulted for historical and biographical background, as well as personal family records.

Books and Dissertations

Baker, Liva. *The Second Battle of New Orleans.* New York, 1996.

Bradford, Roark. *Let the Band Play Dixie.* New York, 1934.

———. *Ol' Man Adam an' His Chillun.* New York, 1928.

Chopin, Kate. *The Awakening.* New York, 1994.

Evans, Eli N. *The Provincials.* New York, 1973.

Fairclough, Adam. *Race and Democracy: The Civil Rights Struggle in Louisiana, 1915–1972.* Athens, Ga., 1995.

Harte, Lillian Bret. *A Handful of Stars.* Hollywood, 1929.

Kane, Harnett T. *Louisiana Hayride.* Gretna, La., 1990.

Leavitt, Mel. *A Short History of New Orleans.* San Francisco, 1982.

Long, Huey P. *Every Man a King: The Autobiography of Huey P. Long.* New Orleans, 1933.

Malone, Bobbie. "Standing 'Unswayed in the Storm': Rabbi Max Heller, Progressivism, and Zionism in the American South, 1860–1929." Ph.D. dissertation, Tulane University, 1994.

St. Martin, Thad. *Madame Toussaint's Wedding Day.* Boston, 1936.

Whitman, Walt. *Leaves of Grass.* New York, 1980.

Williams, T. Harry. *Huey Long.* New York, 1981.

Interviews

Dreyfous, Ruth. Personal interviews, 1992–94.

Weiss, Caroline Dreyfous. Personal interviews, 1992–94.

———. Transcript of oral history by Dorothy Schlesinger. April 11, 1974.

Legal Documents

Weiss v. *United States.* F.2nd 675 #9735. Circuit Court of Appeals, Fifth Circuit.
    September 11, 1941.
Weiss v. *United States. Federal Reporter,* 2nd series. June 9, 1941.

Letters

Dreyfous, Abel. Letters. 1849–90.
Dreyfous, Felix Jonathan. Letter to Caroline D. Weiss. August 9, 1939. Other letters
    and papers.
Dreyfous, Ruth. Letters and papers.
Weiss, Caroline Dreyfous. Letters and papers.
Weiss, Leon Charles. Letters and papers.

Typescripts

Dreyfous, Felix J. Typed autobiography.
Dreyfous, Ruth. "It's Been Very Interesting: My Life." 1993.
Gregory, Angela. Transcript of speech presented September 13, 1982.
Schwab, Thomas. "George Abel Dreyfous: An Appreciation." 1990.
————. "Mathilde Mendelson Schwab: An Appreciation." 1992.
Weiss, Leon. Library speech. N.d.

Newspapers

Baton Rouge *State Times/Morning Advocate.* May 16, 1932.
Item-Tribune (New Orleans). April 21, 1935.
New Orleans *Item.* March 8, April 13, 1939, February 21, 1952.
New Orleans *States.* February 21, 1952.
New York *Times.* Rotogravure picture section. N.d.
Times-Picayune (New Orleans). July 24, 25, 26, 27, 28, 29, 30, 31, August 1, 8, 11, 15,
    22, October 1, 7, 1939, April 23, 1991, p. 1B.
Various undated and unidentified clippings in family collections.

Pamphlets

Art and Architecture at the Lakefront Airport. Prepared by Joan Maloney for the fiftieth
    anniversary of the airport. February 9, 1984.
Board of Commissioners of the Orleans Levee District. *Shushan Airport: Commem-
    orating the Formal Opening.* Summer, 1933. New Orleans.

Historic New Orleans Collection. *The Long Weekend.* Brochure of an exhibition held at the Historic New Orleans Collection, May 11–August 21, 1993.

Louisiana Arts and Sciences Center. *Old Governor's Mansion.* Baton Rouge, 1962.

Louisiana State Capitol: Inaugural and Dedicatory Ceremonies: Official Program. Baton Rouge, May 16, 1932.

Louisiana Tourist Development Commission. *Louisiana Capitol Guide.* Baton Rouge, n.d.

Wurzlow, Helen Emmelin. *Louisiana, Its Capitol.* Baton Rouge, 1932.

Articles and Periodicals

"The Capitol at 50." *Legacy: Louisiana State Archives and Records Service Newsletter* [Baton Rouge]. February, 1982.

Cappel, Glenn. "Five Story Building Moved on 600 Steel Spools." *Engineering News-Record,* October 24, 1935.

Cohn, David L. "Green Pastures for 'Brad.'" *New Orleans Times-Picayune States Magazine,* January 16, 1949.

Deutsch, Hermann B. "Wild Vittles I Have Et." *Saturday Evening Post,* June 10, 1939, p. 33.

Kahn, Catherine. "The Youngest Daughter of Heaven Born Charity." *Touro Views* (Summer, 1990), 13–15.

"Louisiana Capitol at Baton Rouge." *Architectural Forum* (December, 1932), 519.

"Views of Louisiana State University and Agricultural and Mechanical College." *University Bulletin* [Baton Rouge], XXIII (September, 1931).

Weiss, Leon. "The Dawning" and "Run on a Bank." *Tulane University Magazine,* II (April 1902), 184–88.

———. "The Relationship between the Architect and the Draftsman." *Pencil Points,* VIII (January, 1927).